All On The Board

All On The Board

INSPIRATIONAL QUOTES
FROM THE TFL
UNDERGROUND DUO

yellow
kite

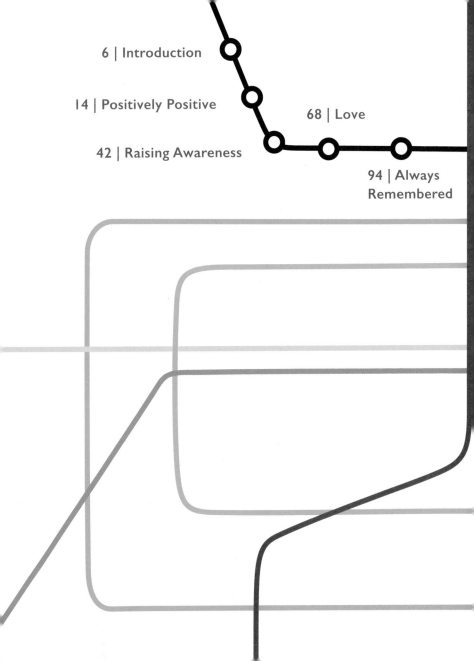

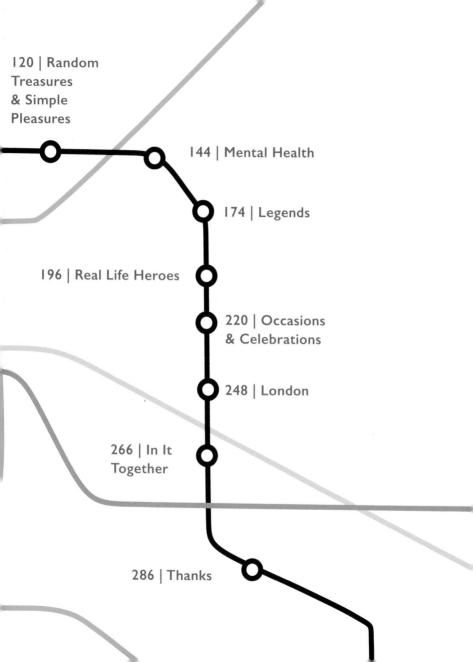

INTRODUCTION

INTRODUCTION

'Once upon a time . . .' is one of many ways we could start this book, but we would much rather say hello. So – hello.

This is the first book we have written, and we hope that's a good way to start it. Let us tell you a little something about ourselves first. This is supposed to be an introduction after all.

There are just two of us behind All On The Board. We are members of staff for the London Underground, working as station assistants during the day and fighting crime (or rather 'writing rhymes') during the night, or any time we feel inspired to.

It all started in March 2017. We were working at North Greenwich station, assisting crowds of Craig David fans through to his concert at The O2 arena. While singing some of his songs to ourselves we started talking about our favourites, and this led us to compose a little poem using some of his song titles and lyrics.

Right in front of us was a customer information board with the words 'KEEP RIGHT' written on it. We thought our poem should be shared with the fans and so we wrote it there and then on that board. It was spontaneous.

After a couple of minutes of it being on display, people were stopping to read it. Each time it was met with a smile and, soon enough, selfies as well. The fans seemed happy, the board seemed happy and it made us feel happy. So we thought 'let's do that again', and we've been writing as a team ever since.

'All on Board' was our original name because it seemed like a welcome to everyone to come on board with us – a statement that we are all in it together. That kind of thing.

After discovering there was already a social media account with that name for a sailing group, we added 'the' and the rest, as they say, is history.

As our popularity grew, we found that more and more people going though North Greenwich station would ask us and other staff, 'Who writes these boards?'

Our answers would often be, 'No one writes them.' Or, 'Everyone writes them.'

So we decided we would call ourselves 'NI' and 'EI'.

Many people think 'NI' and 'EI' are the postcodes where we live, or where we were born, but it just stands for 'No one' and 'Everyone'. Together we could even be 'NEI' – anyone (that's quite clever actually).

We had now become characters through the boards, and that made us realise that when there were large events on we could also have a voice beyond the poetry, and so we moved into writing about mental health plus the health conditions that we both have and also sharing original quotes and words of inspiration or humour – to try and brighten people's days and spread some positivity and joy wherever we could.

Are we experts on health conditions? Are we counsellors? Are we self-help gurus? Absolutely not. We are writing from our own experiences to spread awareness. Yes, we write about conditions that we don't have too, but we always research them and work hard to be as accurate as possible.

As we increased the number of boards, people began to think we were an entire department, so we set up a social media account and introduced ourselves, explaining a bit about what we do, about why we started All On The Board and shared details of our own personal conditions. We wore masks in order to stay anonymous, even though we never expected the level of popularity that came with all of this, but being anonymous was important to allow us to do our day jobs while continuing to write the boards before and after work. The masks were the cheapest disguises we could find at the time, and so we stuck with them.

Along the way we have met celebrities like the comedian Micky Flanagan and Steps, and superstars like Katy Perry and Mumford & Sons have taken selfies with our boards after travelling by Tube in order to see them.

In just three years, we've grown a community of well over 500,000 wonderful followers, and we've appeared in national newspapers, on the television and the radio too. We have been called 'The Banksys of the Underground' and 'The Masked Duo' which we love. Especially being called 'The Masked Duo' because we are huge *Batman* fans.

All On The Board has always been just the two of us. It's a second full-time job we both love to do, even though we don't get paid for it. Being creative is who we are – using creativity to share important messages is a choice. All On The Board is the result, the means to remind others that, as lonely as they may feel sometimes, they really are not alone. To us, it's a simple truth that we are all on this planet together, so let's all get along with each other.

We hope you enjoy this book just as much as we have enjoyed creating it.

Thanks for being you.

All On The Board x

○ @AllontheBoard

f @AllontheBoard

🐦 @AllontheBoard

Love from Our Community

'All On The Board bring joy daily! A chance to stop and read something that could change your day for the better. A much-needed personal touch for busy, bustling, often stressful mornings. I love reading their daily posts.'

– FEARNE COTTON

'During the darkest days of lockdown your positively uplifting words never failed to put a smile on my face. Thank you for the inspiration and love that you spread. Don't ever stop lifting us with your unique brand of joy and humour.'

– TESS DALY

'I love you guys. Thank you for all you do. You both are so appreciated and respected in more ways than one by all of us.'

'The All On The Board Instagram and always apt words are as much as part of the heart of this city as the Thames. I adore all they do and all they stand for.'

– LAUREN MAHON

'Your boards matter and they save lives. You should know that.'

'All On The Board just show how much we need to feel connected . . . you often say exactly what we need to hear at exactly the right time. Always positive, always kind. You make me smile. Sometimes you've made me cry. Keep doing what you are doing . . . we are so very grateful for you.'

– DAVINA MCCALL

'Had a panic attack this morning and then I saw your board. Helped me to remind myself that I'm not alone. A big thank you.'

'All On The Board is a platform that inspires and motivates. A much-welcomed space in the midst of the hustle and bustle to reflect and be uplifted.'

– LAURA WHITMORE

'You guys are amazing! Fighting your own battles but still out here spreading positivity and good vibes for us all!'

'Thank you for reminding us all how powerful words can be, how important empowering others is. Thank you for encouraging and supporting our city, and by that, I mean our people.'

'All On The Board manage to put a smile on thousands of people's faces every day. An iconic symbol of the city I love – I was exploding with excitement when I saw a board supporting campaigns close to me (from dancing to bowel cancer) and championing health awareness. Not only do the messages lift the nation, they are actually saving lives – one board at a time.'

– DEBORAH JAMES

It's so hard to be positive when you feel like everything is going wrong. Sometimes you start thinking that a higher force pulling the strings has some grudge against you personally and is causing your misery. Millions of people feel and think exactly the same thing at times: why is it always me?

You are definitely not alone. Terrible things happen in the world, they always have and they always will. But there are many beautiful things in life that we can focus on, and there are so many things for us to be grateful for.

Millions of people use the Tube every day and mainly keep themselves to themselves. If we smile at one another, or strike up a conversation with a stranger, it is seen as out of the ordinary. That's why, when we write our messages on the boards, it's uplifting to see people stop to read them.

We witness people smiling at or taking photos of the board, standing next to them taking snaps and discussing the quote or poem that has been written on it. It seems to bring people together at the end of a journey in which they may have travelled alone.

I'm constantly writing poems or stories for people I know personally and for those I don't know, with the intention of letting them know that they are loved and they are not alone.

If we can make someone smile, laugh, feel positive, feel motivated, feel better or think about someone or something, then that is truly a wonderful thing.

I love reading positive quotes. They can really make a difference to people and change our outlook on a situation. Words of empathy and reassurance remind you that you're not alone. I adore words that remind me that tomorrow may very well be a better day and, if it isn't, then there's always the day after tomorrow or the day after that. Whenever it arrives, there is a better day. Always.

That's the underlining message we hope our words and boards give to other people. No one knows why we are on this earth, but for as long as we are on it, let's be positively positive for ourselves and for each other whenever we can.

You are reading this because of positivity. The very moment we created All On The Board was a choice between doing it or not doing it. Every reason to do it was positive, and every reason not to was negative. We had a moment to choose; we chose the positive option, and here we are and here you are. Always choose the positive option.

We all have the ability to be positive, and to spark it in those around us, but positivity can be the most elusive of attitudes. You have to work hard to keep it with you, and it can be lost in a flash.

I'm not an expert but I can tell you that being creative is positive. So is love. Be creative, love the people around you, and put them together whenever you can.

We are lucky to be alive at a time where inspirational slogans and mantras are constantly shared across the globe on social media. Social media itself can be an overwhelming place though, remember to hold on tight to the words that lift you up and ring true, the ones that feel important and put them in your pocket for the days when you need them most.

In my life I have had ups and downs, some of those downs have felt or been huge at the time but what Friedrich Nietzsche said really is true; 'That which does not kill us makes us stronger' and if my worst moments have taught me anything it's that I am still here despite them, and so are you. Our worst days can feel like the most impossible wall to climb, with every ladder and climbing assist taken from us as we try to keep climbing.

When I was a child, I wanted to make the world better somehow. I didn't know how I would do it, I just knew I wanted to. It was a very general idea that many would laugh at. It's always been there, even when it became increasingly difficult to obtain as the realities of life took their toll, but by not giving in I found I was telling the world no, that the negative 'truths' and 'reality' were only hurdles and to beat them all I had to do was refuse to fall. It's that determination and refusal that has got me here. I can promise you I would not be here writing these words if I hadn't realised that.

Service information

Date

Time **Be yourself**

Don't change

who you are or

what you believe,

To try to fit in

and make people care;

Just be yourself

because you're amazing

And those who love you

will always be there.

@allontheboard

Service information

Date

Time

MY PROBLEMS
ARE LIKE LEAD BALLOONS
THAT I'VE BEEN
HOLDING ON TO
FOR FAR TOO LONG,
MY HAND IS GRIPPED
TIGHTLY AROUND
THE STRINGS
AND I DON'T KNOW WHY;
IT'S TIME FOR ME TO
SEE AND BELIEVE IN MY HEAD
THAT THEY ARE FILLED
WITH HELIUM INSTEAD OF LEAD,
THEN MAYBE I COULD
LET THEM GO AND WATCH
MY ANXIETIES FLOAT AWAY
ON THE BREEZE AND
INTO THE SKY. @allontheboard

Service information

Hope your
day is as beautiful
as you are...
Which would
be impossible.

@allontheboard

Service information

DON'T GIVE UP

Don't suffer in silence, if you need to,
                    PLEASE SHOUT,
Open up with your feelings, don't be ashamed
                            TO REACH OUT;
Never beat yourself up and know
                        YOU'RE WORTHWHILE,
Tomorrow could be better and
                    YOU MAY FIND YOUR SMILE.
Get help if you need it, don't ever
                        FEEL TOO PROUD,
If you're feeling lonely and
                    LIKE A GHOST IN A CROWD;
Vent your frustrations, don't be
                        FRIGHTENED TO TALK,
Every road has a turn off, for you to walk.

Understand that you're special and
                    BETTER DAYS WILL COME ALONG;
Please know that you are not alone,
                IN TRYING TO BE STRONG.

@allontheboard

Service information

KINDNESS MAKES YOU THE MOST BEAUTIFUL
PERSON IN THE WORLD,
NO MATTER WHAT YOU LOOK LIKE.

THE PROBLEM ISN'T WITH YOUR BODY,
THE PROBLEM IS WHAT
YOU THINK OF IT AND YOURSELF;

DON'T FILTER YOUR FEELINGS
OR LET YOUR REFLECTION BE DISTORTED
BY SOCIETY'S IDEA OF BEAUTY,

BY COMPARING YOURSELF TO
PHOTOS ONLINE OR IN
MAGAZINES ON A SHELF.

@allontheboard

UNDERGROUND

Service information

Date

Time

Don't let the sky be the limit
There's so much space above;
Stand up for what's right,
When push comes to shove.

Don't let decisions be a prison,
Fight for the freedom of choice;
Don't just dream while you're sleeping,
Know the true power of your voice.

@allontheboard

Service information

Date DREAM
CREATE
Time MOTIVATE

PLEASE JUST DO IT, DON'T BE SCARED OF WHAT CAN GO WRONG,
STAND UP AND BE COUNTED, FOLLOW YOUR DREAMS AND BE STRONG;
THERE IS NOTHING WORSE THAN DOING NOTHING AT ALL,
THE BEST LESSON WE CAN LEARN IS HOW TO RISE WHEN WE FALL.
THE ONLY THINGS WORTH FIGHTING FOR ARE LOVE
                          AND THE FREEDOM OF CHOICE;
BELIEVE IN YOURSELF, IN WHAT YOU DO AND
                          HAVE CONVICTION IN YOUR VOICE.
FOCUS ON THE POSITIVES AND LESS ABOUT THE NEGATIVES,
FORGET ABOUT THE THINGS YOU THINK YOU LACK;
BREAK DOWN THE WALLS,
                CHALLENGE THE FEAR OR THE CAUSE,
ITS ONLY YOURSELF THAT IS HOLDING YOU BACK.
ON CLOSE INSPECTION, EVERYONE HAS IMPERFECTIONS,
IN THE THINGS THAT WE SAY AND DO;
LET NOBODY PUT YOU DOWN AND
                SAY YOU'RE NOT GOOD ENOUGH.
BECAUSE YOU'RE PERFECT AT BEING YOU.
CREATE, DON'T DESTROY, EXERCISE AND ENJOY,
PUT PEN TO PAPER AND LEARN;
EDUCATE YOUR MIND TO LEAVE YOUR WORRIES BEHIND,
AND MAY THE FIRE IN YOUR HEART CONTINUE TO BURN.

@allontheboard

Service information

FRIDAY FEELING?

by @allontheboard

YOU CAN'T SEE IT, HEAR IT, SMELL IT OR TASTE IT,
BUT, IT DEFINITELY EXISTS;
YOU CAN'T HOLD IT IN YOUR HANDS,
AND YET IT MAKES PEOPLE PUMP THEIR FISTS.
NO PRESENTS ARE GIFTED, BUT, A WEIGHT IS LIFTED,
THE FREEDOM OF TWO DAYS OFF WORK;
THEY CAN BE FILLED BY LAZING ABOUT,
                        BEING CHILLED OUT,
OR BEING WILD AND RESPONSIBLY BERSERK.
THERE ARE FEELINGS THAT CAN BE IDENTIFIED,
LIKE LOVE, ANGER, DEPRESSION, HATE OR FEAR;
EVEN THOUGH THE FRIDAY FEELING
                        GETS SOME OF US EXCITED,
IT'S AN EMOTION THAT ISN'T TOTALLY CLEAR.

@allontheboard

Service information

HAPPINESS

by @allontheboard

TREAT EVERYONE WITH KINDNESS, INCLUDING YOURSELF,
THERE IS ALWAYS SOMETHING TO BE GRATEFUL FOR;
ENJOY THE LITTLE THINGS IN LIFE,
　　　　　THAT MAY SOMETIMES PASS YOU BY,
CHERISH PRECIOUS MOMENTS AND THOSE WHO YOU ADORE
SPREAD HAPPINESS LIKE BUTTER,
　　　　　OPEN THE BLINDS AND THE SHUTTERS,
RAISE THE CURTAIN ON THE THINGS
　　　　　THAT BRING YOU SMILES;
FROM FASHION TO MUSIC, FOOTBALL TO FOOD,
PIANO PLAYING CATS OR PHOTOS OF HARRY STYLES.
BE COOL WITH WHO YOU ARE AND
　　　　　KNOW YOU'RE A PART OF SOMETHING BIG,
HAVE GOALS TO KEEP LEARNING NEW THINGS;
LIFE CAN BE SWINGS AND ROUNDABOUTS, BUT THE WORLD
IS YOUR PLAYGROUND,
JOY CAN MAKE YOU FLY WITHOUT WINGS.
FIND WAYS TO GET UP, FIND A DISCO TO GET DOWN,
ON EARTH WE ARE ALL SISTERS AND BROTHERS;
IF COMPASSION IS IN YOUR PLAN OF ACTION,
　　　　　YOU MAY GAIN SATISFACTION,
AND BRING HAPPINESS TO YOURSELF AND MANY OTHERS.

@allontheboard

Service information

Date

Time

Just in case nobody
has told you how
special you are today
we thought we would.

YOU ARE SPECIAL

Yes, we mean you.

Keep being you.

@allontheboard

Service information

Monday is
just another day,

They make up
one seventh of our lives

So let's not
wish our lives away.

A Monday can be
whatever you want it to be,

With a little bit of
kindness and positivity.

@allontheboard

Service information
MUNDANE
MONDAY

HERE WE GO AGAIN,
     IT'S THAT DAY THAT STARTS WITH MON,
IT DOESN'T MEAN THAT YOU CAN'T HAVE FUN;
CHECK YOUR LOTTERY NUMBERS,
       JUST IN CASE YOU'VE WON,
EAT A CHEEKY CREAM BUN AND
     DREAM OF A HOLIDAY IN THE SUN.
DON'T WORRY ABOUT THE THINGS
       THAT YOU DIDN'T GET DONE,
JUST TWERK WHILE YOU WORK
      TO THIS WEEK'S NUMBER ONE;
SO, IF YOU HAVE THE MONDAY BLUES,
      BUY A NEW PAIR OF SHOES,
IT WILL SOON BE THE DAY THAT STARTS OFF WITH TUES.
THERE'S NO NEED FOR SAD EMOJIS, AND
       THERE'S NO NEED TO CRY;
BEFORE YOU KNOW IT, YOU CAN BE HAPPY AND
     SHOW IT, WHEN THE DAY BEGINS
         WITH FRI.

@allontheboard

Service information

Date
Time

Every disappointing moment makes it
hard to see,
that it's one step forward
and a small victory;
On closer inspection
Every disappointing rejection,
takes you one step closer
to where you are meant to be.

@allontheboard

Service information

Date

Time

IF YOU AIM FOR PERFECTION
        EACH AND EVERY TIME,
YOU MAY BE DISAPPOINTED
            WITH HOW YOU DO;
IT'S PERFECTLY ALRIGHT
        TO JUST BE GOOD ENOUGH,
AFTER ALL, YOU ARE PERFECT
            AT BEING YOU.

@allontheboard

Service information

Be proud of
who YOU are;
there may be
a long way to go,
But, you've already
come so far.

@allontheboard

Service information

The Future You
is looking back at

The Present You,
thinking

'I'm glad the
tough times are in
the past and I'm
proud of how strong
I was to get through'

@allontheboard

Service information

Date
Time

THE JOURNEY

I'M PRETTY SURE I'M GETTING THERE,
WHEREVER THERE MAY BE;
THE SCENERY MAY CHANGE SOMETIMES,
BUT, I'M STILL THE SAME OLD ME.
I TRY TO PAY ATTENTION TO EACH SIGN.
AND MAKE USE OF ALL THE BREAKS;
THE JOURNEY IS AS IMPORTANT AS THE DESTINATION,
NO MATTER HOW LONG IT TAKES.

THROUGH BETTER AND WORSE,
                THERE'S NO POINT TO REVERSE,
AS I CONTINUE IN A FORWARD MOTION;
BUT, AT THE END OF EVERY OPEN ROAD,
THERE WILL ALWAYS BE A SEA OR AN OCEAN.

@allontheboard

Service information

Date **THINGS WILL**
Time **GET BETTER**

HELLO TO THE PERSON READING THIS.
YOU MAY BE GOING THROUGH A
REALLY TOUGH TIME AT THE MOMENT,
YOU MAY NOT FEEL WORTHWHILE AND
THINK THERE IS NO WAY OUT OF THE
SITUATION YOU ARE IN AND BELIEVE
THINGS WON'T GET BETTER.

YOU ARE WORTHWHILE.

YOU ARE SPECIAL.

YOU ARE NOT ALONE.

THINGS WILL GET BETTER.

@allontheboard

Service information

Date

Time

TREAT YOURSELF
LIKE YOU WOULD
TREAT A GOOD FRIEND;
BECAUSE YOU
SPEND THE MOST TIME
WITH YOURSELF
IN THE END.

@allontheboard

Service information

Date

Time

DON'T THINK
YOU'RE BEING WEAK,
FOR SOMETIMES
WANTING TO HIDE AWAY;
YOU ARE TIRED
FROM BEING STRONG,
IT TAKES STRENGTH
TO FACE THE WORLD
EVERY DAY.

@allontheboard

Service information

LIFE
DOESN'T ALWAYS
GO TO PLAN,
JUST KEEP GOING
AND
DO WHAT YOU CAN,
LOVE YOURSELF
AND BE YOUR OWN
BIGGEST FAN.

@allontheboard

Service information

Date

Time

IF MONEY
        IS WORTH SAVING
AND TIME
        IS WORTH SAVING
YOU ARE
        MORE THAN
                WORTH SAVING.

@allontheboard

Nobody is perfect. What is 'perfect' anyway?

Every one of us has something that we have to deal with at some point in our lives with regards to health. It may be something we are born with, something which develops over time, or something which suddenly happens to us. Some conditions are life-threatening and others are a nuisance. Either way, we all have our own personal battles to fight.

Some conditions can be seen but then there are those which are invisible. I was diagnosed with ulcerative colitis in 2011. It has changed how I live and is challenging at times, but I'm determined to not let it get the better of me, even if there seems to be periods of time when it does.

I have good days and I have bad days, like we all do. Even though there are times when I have pain, I do not class myself or label myself as suffering with ulcerative colitis. I live my life the best I can with some changes and adjustments.

When I go to places, I don't feel comfortable until I know where the nearest toilets are. I always try to get an aisle seat if I'm travelling or at any concert or event, so I can get to a toilet as quickly as possible. I have to be quick to adapt to new environments.

There are many other symptoms that come with ulcerative colitis. One of the hardest to deal with is the chronic fatigue. Sometimes I may look as fit as a fiddle (not often), yet inside I only feel fit to drop. I've been accused of being lazy at times when every step has felt like a mile.

Because a condition may be invisible, often people think that it isn't there. We have written boards for our own conditions because we know about them from experience, but we have also written boards about other health conditions and invisible illnesses after researching them.

We do try our best to raise awareness, and to let people know that they are not the only ones suffering out there in the world. Like I said, I have ulcerative colitis, but it doesn't have me. I will not let it have me, no matter how difficult it gets.

Whichever health condition you have, we hope you feel (or can start to feel) the same way too.

We are all mortal, and our health reminds us of this the most. Many people in this world have health conditions that bring them discomfort, and most of these conditions are not recognised by others around them who can't see that pain. We suffer in silence and on the outside look 'normal'. There is injustice in this, and if we could all learn to comprehend the internal pains of others better then we can support each other.

I have tinnitus. Tinnitus is a sound in my head that won't go away, mostly on my left side. Everyone who has it hears a different sound, and some hear multiple sounds. Mine is a high-pitched drone – as if someone had hit a suspended steel triangle and let it ring forever. At times it's debilitating, and it can cause disturbed sleep and concentration, as well as a loss of patience. When I write I also listen to music, and my concentration is infinitely better. There is no cure.

I manage this condition with music – I listen to a playlist of film scores from my favourite composers: Hans Zimmer, Ennio Morricone and John Barry, among others. Occasionally, when it's really bad, I look for drone-like sounds to mix to the same frequency as my tinnitus to 'drown it out'. I try this with headphones when I need to sleep.

If you've seen the movie *Baby Driver* then you'll know how important music can be in controlling tinnitus, and unlocking who you are in the process. It certainly does that for me.

I have tinnitus. It doesn't have me.

Of course, you wouldn't know if I, or anyone else, had tinnitus, but I know I am not alone with it. It's just one condition I have, and you may have conditions too; I hope you are able to manage yours and get the help you need. Over 95 per cent of people on the planet have a health concern of some kind, about half of which are chronic. Those numbers alone mean that we can significantly change the world for the better if we each simply recognise that the stranger in front of us potentially has something that requires understanding and empathy.

You may struggle with something that very few people know anything about, and it's for this reason we work hard on raising awareness of the many physical and mental health conditions that exist. This chapter is a collection of some of those we have written about. One day we hope to have covered them all.

Service information

Date **A HARD**

Time **CONFESSION**

IT MAY BE A HARD CONFESSION TO SAY
    YOU'RE STRUGGLING WITH THE ILLNESS
        THAT LIVES WITH YOU;
AT TIMES IT MAY FEEL LONELY,
    YOU MAY FEEL LIKE THE ONE AND ONLY,

BUT, THERE ARE MILLIONS OF PEOPLE
    WHO KNOW WHAT YOU'RE GOING THROUGH.
TOGETHER WE CAN BE STRONG AND
    HELP EACH OTHER GET ALONG,

DON'T LET THE CONDITIONS WE HAVE
    KILL OUR LOVE AND HOPE;

WHENEVER WE DON'T FEEL FINE,
    THERE ARE PHONE NUMBERS TO CALL

WITH PEOPLE AT THE OTHER END OF THE LINE,
THE PURPOSE OF HUMANITY IS TO
    HELP ONE ANOTHER COPE.

@allontheboard

Service information

Date WORLD
Time AIDS DAY

AIDS CANNOT BE SPREAD BY A HUG OR A HANDSHAKE

OR HAVING A MEAL WITH A FRIEND;

RAISE AWARENESS AND BRING ATTENTION

        TO THE CAUSE AND THE PREVENTION

AND FIGHT FOR THE DISEASE TO COME TO AN END

NEVER SHOW IGNORANCE, LIVE WITHOUT PREJUDICE

AND NEVER LOSE HOPE, FOR SURE;

BE SAFE WITH EDUCATION, TAKE MEDICATION

        AND SHOW DEDICATION.

NEVER GIVE UP ON EACH OTHER

        OR TO FIND A CURE.

@allontheboard

Service information

Date

Time

CANCER DOESN'T CARE

CANCER DOESN'T CARE IF YOU ARE ROYALTY
OR A KARDASHIAN,

A FOOTBALLER, A MODEL, A FILM STAR OR ON TV;
CANCER DOESN'T CARE IF YOU HAVE BEEN
AT NUMBER ONE IN THE CHARTS,

IT TRULY DOESN'T CARE IF IT HURTS YOU AND ME.
CANCER DOESN'T CARE ABOUT WHO WE ARE OR
THE COLOUR OF OUR SKIN,

IT DOESN'T MATTER WHERE WE LIVE OR WHAT WE DO;
CANCER DOESN'T CARE IF IT AFFECTS ONE IN TWO PEOPLE,

IF IT'S NOT ME, THEN IT COULD VERY WELL BE YOU.

CANCER DOESN'T CARE WHAT YOU BELIEVE IN
OR IF YOU'RE YOUNG OR OLD,

IT DOESN'T CARE IF YOU'RE A CHILD,
A FATHER OR A MOTHER;

CANCER DOESN'T CARE ABOUT US,
IT PROVES IT TIME AFTER TIME

SO, LET'S CARE ABOUT OURSELVES AND ONE ANOTHER.

@allontheboard

Service information

Date **CHRONIC**

Time TO BE ME

This CHRONIC pain is driving me crazy,
When I've got CHRONIC fatigue
I'm not being lazy;
I have a CHRONIC condition
which nobody can see,
There are times in my life
when it feels
CHRONIC to be me.

@allontheboard

Service information

Date

Time DIABETES

THERE ARE GOOD DAYS AND THERE ARE BAD DAYS

AND ALTHOUGH DIABETES IS LIFE-CHANGING,

ALMOST EVERYTHING YOU DID BEFORE

YOU CAN STILL DO;

YOU ARE STRONG AND YOU CAN DO THIS,

AT TIMES IT'S HARD, BUT YOU'RE NOT ALONE;

IF YOU'RE TYPE 1 OR TYPE 2

YOU ARE MORE THAN YOUR CONDITION

AND IT DOESN'T DEFINE YOU.

@allontheboard

Service information

Date **CROHN'S**

Time **& COLITIS**

THE WORRY, THE DEPRESSION, THE ANXIETY,
STRESSING AND OBSESSING ABOUT WHERE THE NEAREST
TOILET MAY BE;
RELAPSES AND FLARE UPS FEEL LIKE VICIOUS TRAPS,
IT TAKES GUTS TO GET BY WHEN YOU FEEL FIT TO COLLAPSE.
DIARRHOEA MIXED WITH BLOOD AND MUCUS
CAN BE A WICKED GAME OF PORCELAIN THRONES;
THE INFLAMMATION AND DEHYDRATION LEAVES ME WEAK
WITH NO ENERGY IN MY FLESH AND BONES.
TIREDNESS AND FATIGUE LEAVES ME BOTTOM OF THE LEAGUE
WITH UNCONTROLLED WEIGHT LOSS AND GAIN;
THIS INVISIBLE ILLNESS NOBODY CAN SEE
LEAVES ME IN CHRONIC PAIN.
TRAVELLING CAN BE A MISSION WITH THIS CONDITION
AND TASKS CAN BE HARD TO COMPLETE;
TO BE ABLE TO REACH THE TOILET IN AN EMERGENCY
I OFTEN NEED AN AISLE SEAT.
IT'S A LIFELONG AND LIFE-CHANGING CONDITION THAT AFFECTS
MY BODY AND MY MOOD;
SO MANY SYMPTOMS PUT ME OFF ACTIVITIES AND FOOD.
SOMETIMES I MAKE EXCUSES WHEN I NEED MY COMFORT ZONE,
IT'S ISOLATING, DEBILITATING AND FRUSTRATING,
BUT, I KNOW I'M NOT ALONE.

@allontheboard

Service information

Date

Time **DEAFNESS**

KINDNESS IS A LANGUAGE WHICH THE DEAF CAN HEAR,
AND THE BLIND CAN ALSO SEE;
DON'T LET COMMUNICATION BARRIERS CAUSE ISOLATION AND DEPRESSION,
OR EXCLUSION FROM SOCIETY.
PEOPLE SAY LOVE IS BLIND, BUT, LOVE IS ALSO DEAF,
YOU CAN'T JUST TELL SOMEONE YOU LOVE THEM, YOU HAVE TO SHOW IT;
SIGNS ARE TO EYES, WHAT WORDS ARE TO EARS,
LIKE A CHORUS TO A SONG, OR RHYMES TO A POET.
PLEASE BE DEAF AWARE AND SHOW THAT YOU CARE, BY USING SOME HELPFUL TIPS;
DON'T LOOK AWAY OR COVER UP YOUR MOUTH, IF SOMEONE IS READING YOUR LIPS.
HAVE THE ATTENTION OF THE PERSON BEFORE YOU START TO SPEAK,
PLACES WITH GOOD LIGHTING ARE BEST FOR A CONVERSATION;
USE PLAIN LANGUAGE, NORMAL LIP MOVEMENTS AND FACIAL EXPRESSIONS,
SIGNING IS AN AWESOME FORM OF COMMUNICATION.
IF THE PERSON DOESN'T UNDERSTAND, THEN TRY A DIFFERENT WAY,
DON'T EVER SAY, 'IT'S NOTHING TO WORRY ABOUT';
KEEP YOUR VOICE DOWN BECAUSE IT'S UNCOMFORTABLE FOR HEARING AID USERS,
IF YOU TALK FAR TOO LOUD OR SHOUT.
WE HAD BODY LANGUAGE BEFORE WE HAD SPEECH,
HANDS CAN BE MOUTHS AND EYES CAN BE EARS;
EVEN THOUGH THEY CAN'T HEAR, DEAF PEOPLE CAN DO ANYTHING,
FROM FACING OBSTACLES TO CONQUERING FEARS.
SIGN LANGUAGE COMES IN HANDY, WHEN THE HEARING WORLD LISTENS,
LIFE CAN BE SO GREAT,
WE CAN MAKE A BIG CHANGE TO PEOPLE'S LIVES WITH TECHNOLOGY,
AND THE WAY WE COMMUNICATE.

@allontheboard

UNDERGROUND

Service information

Date
Time CHRONIC ILLNESS

by @allontheboard

IT WILL NOT BEAT ME,
IT SHALL NOT DEFEAT ME,
JUST BECAUSE IT LIVES
WITH ME,
IT DOESN'T COMPLETE ME.

@allontheboard

Service information

Date **Down**

Time **Syndrome**

ONE EXTRA CHROMOSOME, CAN CREATE AN EXTRA LOVING HOME,
LOVE IS THE GREATEST GIFT THAT WE CAN GIVE;
A DISABILITY DOESN'T DEFINE A PERSON, DON'T CHANGE ANYONE
FOR THE WORLD,
JUST CHANGE THE WORLD FOR EVERYONE TO LIVE.

SMILES ARE CONTAGIOUS, LAUGHTER IS INFECTIOUS,
LOVE AND HUGS CAN BRING JOY TO THE HEART;
DOWN SYNDROME HAPPENED RANDOMLY, LIKE WINNING THE LOTTERY,
IT'S A JOURNEY SOME MAY NEED SOME HELP TO START.

A NEGATIVE SOCIETY AFFECTS THE QUALITY OF LIFE,
MORE THAN HAVING DOWN SYNDROME EVER CAN;
THEY DO NOT 'SUFFER FROM IT' OR ARE 'AFFLICTED WITH IT',
THEY CAN STUDY, GET MARRIED, HAVE CAREERS AND ALSO A PLAN.

DON'T JUDGE SOMEONE BASED ON DIAGNOSIS,
DON'T LABEL THEM WITH WHAT YOUR EYES MIGHT PERCEIVE;
DON'T MISS OUT ON THEIR BEAUTY AND ABILITIES,
JUST WITNESS WHAT THEY CAN ACHIEVE.

@allontheboard

Service information

Date ENDOMETRIOSIS

Time

By @allontheboard

ENDOMETRIOSIS AFFECTS MORE THAN 1 IN 10 WOMEN IN THE WORLD,
IT'S ONE OF THE MOST PAINFUL HEALTH CONDITIONS ACCORDING TO THE NHS;
THERE IS A LACK OF AWARENESS FOR THIS CHRONIC CONDITION AND NO CURE,
IT WREAKS HAVOC ON WOMEN'S LIVES AND RELATIONSHIPS WITH PAIN AND STRESS.
TISSUE RESEMBLING THE LINING OF THE UTERUS GROWS ON THE WRONG SIDE,
CAUSING SCARRING, LESIONS, ADHESIONS, OVARIAN AND OTHER CYSTS;
WE MAY NOT BE ABLE TO SEE IT AND THE PERSON SUFFERING MIGHT NOT LOOK SICK,
BUT, IT'S AN INVISIBLE ILLNESS THAT MOST CERTAINLY EXISTS.
IT'S HARD TO SUFFER IN SILENCE WHEN THE SYMPTOMS MAKE YOU WANT TO SCREAM,
FEELING SICK AND EXHAUSTED, STRUGGLING TO CARRY ON WITH HOW YOU FEEL;
50% OF WOMEN WITH ENDOMETRIOSIS HAVE DIFFICULTY BECOMING PREGNANT,
SOME PEOPLE SHOW THEIR SCARS TO LET OTHERS KNOW THEY CAN HEAL.
IT'S A CHRONIC ILLNESS CAUSING EMOTIONAL AND MENTAL STRESS
                                                        WITH PHYSICAL PAINS;
AGONISING PELVIC CRAMPING AND OVULATION, PAINFUL BOWEL MOVEMENTS
                                                        AND URINATION,
INFLAMMATIONS, VOMITING, NAUSEA AND ALSO MIGRAINES.
DIGESTIVE PROBLEMS, BLOATED STOMACHS, IRREGULAR AND HEAVY BLEEDING
                                    MAY CAUSE EMBARRASSING MOMENTS,
BLOOD CLOTS, SPOTTING, MOOD SWINGS, BRAIN FOGGING, NIGHT SWEATS AND
                                                PAIN WITH INTERCOURSE;
IT WOULD BE NICE TO LIVE AND WORK WITHOUT CONSTANT FATIGUE,
                                        FEELING DOWNBEAT AND HURT,
OR IN THE FOETAL POSITION LIKE YOU'VE BEEN KICKED BY A HORSE.
SURGERY DOESN'T ALWAYS GUARANTEE ANY EASE FROM THE SYMPTOMS,
MEDICATION FOR THE PAIN MAY HELP YOU WHEN YOUR HEART SINKS LIKE A STONE;
DURING NIGHTS OF BEING DOUBLED OVER IN PAIN, GRITTING YOUR TEETH,
                    HEAT PADS AND HOT WATER BOTTLES MAY BRING SOME RELIEF,
AS LONELY AS IT FEELS IN THAT MOMENT, PLEASE KNOW YOU ARE NOT ALONE.

@allontheboard

Service information

Date EPILEPSY

Time _____

EACH PERSON WITH EPILEPSY IS DIFFERENT,
THERE ARE SO MANY TYPES OF SEIZURES,
IT'S MORE THAN FALLING TO THE FLOOR AND STARTING TO SHAKE;
DURING THE DARKNESS NEVER LOSE SIGHT OF HOPE,
EVERY SETBACK SEEMS LIKE A SLIPPERY SLOPE,
SOMETIMES IT FEELS LIKE IT'S JUST TOO MUCH TO TAKE.
EPILEPSY IS AN UNPREDICTABLE SHADOW, NEVER GIVING
ANY WARNING OF WHEN IT WILL ATTACK,
LEAVING SOMEONE FEELING ANXIOUS AND FULL OF DREAD;
IT ISN'T CONTAGIOUS, BUT IT CAN BE DANGEROUS
TO RESTRAIN SOMEONE DURING THE SEIZURE,
MAKE SURE TO PUT SOMETHING SOFT UNDER THEIR HEAD.
THERE IS A SUPERHERO IN EACH OF US, EVEN IF WE
DON'T WEAR CAPES,
A TRUE HERO SHOULD BE MEASURED BY THE SIZE OF THEIR HEART;
EPILESPY TRIES TO STEAL ENERGY AND HEALTH,
BUT, IT CAN'T TAKE AWAY HOPE, FAITH AND LOVE,
EVEN IF IT MAKES SOMEONE FEEL THEIR SOUL AND BODY HAVE DRIFTED APART.
AN AURA BEFORE A SEIZURE MAY INCLUDE SCARY VISUAL CHANGES,
FROM BRIGHT LIGHTS, ZIG ZAGS, DARKNESS AND DISTORTED ILLUSION;
NAUSEA WITH ANXIETY AND FEAR, NUMBNESS AND
TINGLING ON ONE SIDE,
AFTER THE BRAIN HAS RECOVERED FROM A SEIZURE,
THERE IS OFTEN CONFUSION.
IT'S A DAILY STRUGGLE BEING IN PAIN OR FEELING SICK INSIDE
WHEN THE WORLD SAYS YOU'RE LOOKING FINE,
IT CAN MAKE YOU FORGET AND AFFECTS YOUR MEMORY;
ANYONE CAN GET EPILEPSY, IT HAS SO MANY TRIGGERS,
BUT, YOU'RE NOT ALONE FACING THIS INVISIBLE ENEMY.

@allontheboard

Service information

Date
Time

YOU MAY FEEL LIKE A JIGSAW PUZZLE,

MISSING A PIECE AND INCOMPLETE;

DON'T LET THE CONDITIONS YOU HAVE DEFINE WHO YOU ARE,

SHINE LIKE A STAR WITH EVERY CHALLENGE YOU MEET.

KNOWLEDGE IS POWER, THERE WILL BE A FINE HOUR,

WHEN YOU LAUGH IN THE FACE OF DEFEAT;

BE PROUD IN THE CROWD, FOR EACH BATTLE SHOUT LOUD,

'I AM ME AND I WILL NOT BE BEAT'.

@allontheboard

UNDERGROUND ## Service information

INVISIBLE

FOR EVERYONE WITH A DISABILITY OR AN ILLNESS
THAT CAN'T BE SEEN

by
@allontheboard

NOT ALL DISABILITIES AND ILLNESSES ARE VISIBLE,
WHEN YOU SAY WHAT YOU'VE GOT, SOME REPLY,
  'BUT, YOU'RE FAR TOO YOUNG AND BEAUTIFUL';
YOU MAY WEAR NICE CLOTHES
   AND HAVE A HEALTHY TAN,
BUT, JUST TO GO OUT FOR THE NIGHT
   REQUIRES A MASTER PLAN.
'WHERE ARE THE NEAREST TOILETS?
  HAVE I GOT MY MEDICATION WITH ME?',
'WILL PEOPLE HELP ME IN AN EMERGENCY?';
SORTING OUT A RELAXING HOLIDAY
   CAN BE A TEST OF ENDURANCE,
FROM WATCHING WHAT YOU EAT
   TO CHOOSING THE RIGHT INSURANCE.
A SMILE CAN HIDE THE DEPRESSION,
   THE FATIGUE AND CHRONIC PAIN,
NOBODY WILL EVER NOTICE THE TEARS
   IF YOU'RE CRYING IN THE RAIN;
JUST BECAUSE WE LOVE TO LAUGH, DANCE AND TAKE A SELFIE
IT DOESN'T MEAN WE HAVE RECOVERED
   AND ARE BACK TO
@allontheboard FEELING HEALTHY.

Service information

Date

Time ___MENOPAUSE___

by @allontheboard

HOT AND COLD FLUSHES, IRRITABILITY AND NIGHT SWEATS,
ITCHY SKIN AND WORSENING OF ALLERGIES;
CLAMMY FEELINGS WITH MOOD SWINGS,
                    FATIGUE AND TROUBLE SLEEPING,
DIZZINESS, VERTIGO AND TINGLING EXTREMITIES.

HAIR LOSS AND THINNING, EARS SOMETIMES RINGING,
A FAULTY MEMORY, LACK OF FOCUS AND POOR CONCENTRATION;
ACHING JOINTS, MUSCLE TENSION AND
                  THINGS TOO SENSITIVE TO MENTION,
HEADACHES, ANXIETY, DEPRESSION, FEELINGS OF DREAD
                      AND HEART PALPITATIONS.

BLEEDING GUMS, BURNING TONGUES,
                  A CHANGE OF ODOUR AND BREATH,
INCONTINENCE, BLOATING, DIGESTIVE ISSUES AND FACIAL HAIR;
FINGERNAILS WEAKEN, A LOSS OF LIBIDO,
                  POSSIBLE OSTEOPOROSIS,
WE CAN'T PRETEND TO KNOW WHAT YOU'RE GOING THROUGH,
        BUT, WE CAN TRY TO SHOW YOU WE CARE.

@allontheboard

Service information

Date MIGRAINES

Time & HEADACHES

by
@allontheboard

THE PAIN CAN BE INTENSE ON ONE SIDE
OR BOTH SIDES OF THE HEAD,
IT CAN AFFECT THE FACE AND ALSO THE NECK,
EVERY MOVEMENT CAN WORSEN THE THROBBING AND PULSATING SENSATION;
FROM FEELING NAUSEOUS TO POSSIBLY BEING SICK,
EXTRA SENSITIVE TO LIGHT AND SOUND,
SWEATING, FEELING HOT OR COLD, STOMACH PAINS,
AND POOR CONCENTRATION.
CHANGES IN BEHAVIOUR, ENERGY LEVELS AND MOOD,
AN APPETITE NOT QUITE RIGHT AND NOT UP FOR EATING FOOD,
THE DIZZINESS AND FEELING OFF BALANCE ARE A CHALLENGE
WHEN FEELING WEAK;
AURAS CAN WARN US OF SOMETHING WAITING TO HAPPEN,
VISUAL PROBLEMS FROM FLASHING LIGHTS TO BLACK SPOTS
AND ZIG-ZAG PATTERNS,
PINS AND NEEDLES UP THE ARMS AND SOMETIMES DIFFICULTY
WHEN TRYING TO SPEAK.
MIGRAINES AND HEADACHES ARE INVISIBLE
AND THE SYMPTOMS CAN LAST FOR HOURS OR DAYS,
THEY CAN LEAVE US CRAVING DARKNESS AND SILENCE,
NEEDING THE COMFORT OF A BED;
IT'S A MENTAL, EMOTIONAL AND PHYSICAL ASSAULT
ON THE BODY,
THE PAIN IS TORTURE WHEN IT'S ALL IN THE HEAD.

@allontheboard

Service information

PERSONAL BATTLES

WE HAVE THE WORLD ON OUR SHOULDERS,
AND STILL TRY TO STAND TALL;
GETTING OUT OF BED CAN BE A CHALLENGE.
AND SOMETIMES WE HIT A BRICK WALL;
WITH OUR UNWELCOME CHRONIC CONDITIONS,
WE ARE TRYING TO FIND OUR WAY;
EVEN THOUGH WE FEEL WEAK,
     WE REALLY MUST BE STRONG,
TO FIGHT OUR PERSONAL BATTLES
                    EACH DAY.

@allontheboard

Service information

Date

Time **PREMATURITY**

THEY FIGHT EVERY DAY TO LIVE AND BREATHE,
WE FIGHT WITH UNCONDITIONAL LOVE AND BECAUSE WE BELIEVE,
ALL BABIES ON EARTH DESERVE TO HAVE A HEALTHY START;
SEEING A PREMATURE BABY FIGHT FOR SURVIVAL
                            IS BOTH TERRIFYING AND LIFE-CHANGING,
AS HELPLESS AS WE FEEL,
WE MUST NEVER LOSE HOPE OR LOSE HEART.
IT'S SCARY, ANXIOUS AND A STRESSFUL TIME WATCHING
    A NEW BORN BABY SURROUNDED BY THE DOCTORS, NURSES,
                                MACHINES AND WIRES,
TINY AND FRAGILE, ARRIVING MUCH SOONER THAN PLANNED;
THEY ARE LITTLE HEROES AS SOON AS THEY ARE BORN,
IT'S COMPLETELY UNDERSTANDABLE
                TO FEEL SAD, ANGRY AND UNSURE
                        HOW TO HANDLE IT ALL,
WHEN WE JUST WANT TO FIGHT THE BATTLE FOR THEM,
TAKE THEM HOME AND HAVE A FINGER GRIPPED BY A TINY HAND.

@allontheboard

Service information

Date TINNITUS by @allantheboard

Time

TINNITUS CAN BE IN ONE EAR, BOTH EARS AND
                    IN THE MIDDLE OF THE HEAD,
IT CAN BE CONTINUOUS AND IT MAY ALSO COME AND GO;
SOME PEOPLE THINK THE NOISE IS COMING FROM OUTSIDE
                        AND TRY TO HUNT IT DOWN,
THE VOLUME, INTENSITY AND PITCH CAN BE HIGH, MEDIUM OR LOW.

TINNITUS CAN BE A LONELY STRUGGLE CAUSING STRESS,
                       ANXIETY AND WORRY,
PHYSICAL TENSION WITH DEPRESSION AND IMPOSSIBLE TO IGNORE;
IT CAN AFFECT CONCENTRATION AND SLEEP,
                   WHEN THERE IS NOT A MOMENTS PEACE,
FROM THE RINGING, HUMMING, WHOOSHING, BUZZING AND ALSO THE ROAR.

TINNITUS CAN AFFECT THOSE WHO ARE EXPOSED TO LOUD MUSIC,
               FROM THE DJ'S, BANDS AND CONCERT GOERS,
TO PEOPLE WITH HEARING LOSS OR WORKING WITH MACHINERY;
EAR WAX BUILD UP, LOUD MUSIC AND EAR INFECTION,
PERFORATED EAR DRUMS AND NO EAR PROTECTION,
TUMOURS, NOISE EXPOSURE, STRESS, VERTIGO AND MÉNIÈRE'S DISEASE.
SILENCE CAN BE VIOLENT TO SOMEONE EXPERIENCING TINNITUS,
WHEN THERE'S A RIOT OF PHANTOM SOUNDS IN THE COMFORT ZONE;
I IN IO IN THE UK HAS THE CONDITION AND
                   MILLIONS MORE AROUND THE WORLD,
THERE IS HELP OUT THERE, PLEASE KNOW YOU'RE NOT ALONE.

Service information

IF YOU STRUGGLE
TO GET OUT OF BED,
BUT, YOU STILL DO,
THEN YOU ARE
TRULY A FIGHTER;
WHEN THE WORLD
GOES DARK ON YOU,
AS WEAK AS YOU FEEL,
YOU WILL FIND
THE STRENGTH TO
SHINE BRIGHTER.

@allontheboard

Making new friends

For probably the first year after we began, we responded to every single comment and message we received. It was a joy to do so because it was very much a part of how we know what to write about, and what matters to those who feel alone. But in 2018 we had a few football fields worth of followers show up and suddenly it became an impossible task to keep up with the demand alongside our day jobs. We haven't stopped trying to respond to as many people as we can, but we now have to randomly look through the messages. Sometimes we stumble on truly beautiful and inspiring comments that prove to us that we are making a genuine difference to people's lives. We wish we could answer every single message, but we hope the poems we write do that just as well.

We constantly do birthday boards for people in the public eye (living and dead) who we admire. We still do them now.

We were doing birthday boards pretty much every day during the lockdown of the pandemic for people born on those dates, and not to any specific people because every day is a birthday to someone and should be celebrated even if a pandemic might think otherwise.

What is love?

According to reliable sources, love doctors all over the world, and the many millions of songs written since the Big Bang happened, LOVE is the greatest thing.

Love is all around us, and all we need is love. The legendary rock star Meatloaf would do anything for it (although we still haven't found out what he wouldn't do for it).

Everybody loves the feeling of being in love, and it feels equally marvellous to be loved.

When you are truly in love with somebody, all you want to do is make them happy. Their happiness makes you happy. You would give them the world if you could, and you would most definitely let them have the last sweet in the packet. Wherever you live, wherever you roam, or however lost you might feel, their heart is your home and you always want to be there.

Just looking at them becomes your favourite view. Their name becomes your favourite word. Their voice is your favourite sound (even if when they sing at karaoke they sound like two cats having an argument over who spilled the saucer of milk). You feel privileged and lucky to share the jokes and that secret language that comes with a relationship, as well as each other's dreams.

Love is flipping fantastic. It can have you doing front flips and back flips, and every flip that is possible to flip while wearing flip flops and flipping pancakes. But, when you lose love, it can be the worst feeling in the world.

Falling in love is easy, but when you are in a relationship it does take effort to make it work. If love is a flower, then it requires water and sunshine to help it grow and to keep it alive. Some days you are the water, some days you may be the sun. If it only gets one of those, or neither, then the flower will wither and die.

But sometimes that's part of life. As sad as it seems, when a relationship ends it means you are one step closer to someone who you are truly meant to be with.

The whole point of life is truly love. Not just the relationship kind of love, but love for family, friends, people and animals. A love for doing things we enjoy. A love for music. A love for a football team. A love for food and drink. A love for travelling. A love for life and laughter.

It's all about love. We live for love.

Is there an emotion that has been written about as much as love?
Is there one that matters as much?

To me, love is magic. It's mysterious; we should never ignore its
pulse and wisdom. And it's everywhere. It's in the trees, in all
animals, in the sounds of birds chirping and the colours of autumn
and the eyes of those I hold dearest. Love for your work can
make it the easiest job on earth; love for a person can make their
soul so recognisable you can find them in the largest of crowds.

Love has the power to lift a person in their weakest moment, or
bring the strongest person to their knees. We know of it, but
not always what it is. We feel it, but often cannot explain why,
there is often no rhyme or reason.

When we write our boards, we write them with love. Even
boards you would think have no connection with love still need
it for them to work. Love gives a genuine voice and creates
an unforgettable description. The pain and darkest fears of
countless conditions need love in order for us to discover the
positive solutions we write about.

As a gift, love is truly the greatest of them all. But you can lose it if you don't look after it. We are all born with a great capacity for love, but life can cloud that power and make it hard to find or see it, even when it's right in front of us.

Love stories can begin in the most unlikely places, even at a Tube station . . . At Canary Wharf, every day commuters queue up in perfect rows along the platform. For 6 months I was positioned by an escalator on the platform to monitor crowding and on my first day I noticed a man who kept giving up his spot to the person behind. It went on for almost 3 trains; he was clearly waiting for something. A lady emerged through the crowd and he smiled. They didn't know each other. Clearly he was wanting to speak with her, but his nerves got the better of him. He did this for the next 4 days. It wasn't until day 5 that he struck up a conversation. Her response seemed kind but by the time the escalator was repaired a matter of weeks later they were both queueing in the same row at the same time every day, blissfully unaware of all the people around them. Love stories unfold all the time on the Tube but this one sticks with me for its patience and the reminder that love can change the most stringent routine so suddenly. It can break barriers set in stone and change your world.

Have you found love? Have you lost it? I hope this chapter will fill you with joy on your journey towards it. Never give up on that journey. If you keep on looking for love in the things around you, then love will find you. Grab it and never let it go. You deserve it. Everyone deserves it.

Service information

When you're with
your Prince or
Princess Charming,
It may seem alarming,
When you look back
at all the frogs
you kissed;
It only goes to show,
A happy ending is possible,
And a fairy tale
can truly exist.

@allontheboard

Service information

BABIES

by @allontheboard

NOTHING CAN BEAT THE FEELING OF MAKING
A BABY SMILE,
OR WHEN WE SEE THE LOOK OF PURE LOVE
IN THEIR EYES;
THE SWEETEST SOUND IN THE WORLD IS
THEIR LAUGHTER OR
WHEN THEY'RE BLOWING RASPBERRIES,
AND WHEN THEY GIGGLE AT A PEEK-A-BOO
THAT TAKES THEM BY SURPRISE.
NOTHING CAN MAKE YOU FEEL AS WANTED
AS WHEN THEY GRIP YOUR FINGER
WITH A TINY HAND,
WE WANT TO DO EVERYTHING WE CAN TO
MAKE THEM HAPPY;
THEY ARE QUICK TO BE FORGIVEN
FOR THE SLEEPLESS NIGHTS AND
LITTLE TANTRUMS,
AND EVERY SMELLY PACKAGE
THEY LEAVE WITH LOVE INSIDE A NAPPY.

Service information

Date
Time CHILDREN

WE HAVE IT IN OUR POWER,

TO HELP EACH ONE TO BLOOM AND BLOSSOM LIKE A FLOWER,

THE CHILDREN ARE THE FUTURE AND THE FUTURE IS NOW;

LET THEM BELIEVE IN MAGIC AND BE FILLED WITH WONDER,

IF THEY CAN'T THEN IT'S US WHO WILL FAIL.

DON'T SHOW THEM VIOLENCE, GIVE THEM LOVE, COMFORT AND GUIDANCE,

SHOW THEM THE DIFFERENCE BETWEEN WHAT'S RIGHT AND WRONG;

A CHILDHOOD SHOULD BE FUN, EACH ONE SHOULD ENJOY BEING YOUNG,

BECAUSE ADULTHOOD CAN BE FAR TOO LONG.

WHATEVER OUR SITUATION, LET THEM ENJOY AN IMAGINATION,

GIVE THEM EDUCATION AND ENCOURAGEMENT TO HELP THEM THRIVE;

WHATEVER CHILDREN NEED, WE CAN HELP THEM TO GROW AND TO SUCCEED,

IT'S DOWN TO US TO KEEP EACH OF THEIR DREAMS ALIVE.

@allontheboard

Service information

Date
Time COMING OUT

Inspired by Jameela Jamil

Add a rainbow to your name,

Come out when you're ready and don't be ashamed,

Everybody should be free to love who they love,

without any fear;

Nobody should have to feel afraid of not being

accepted by their community,

Or worried about how their sexuality

may damage their career.

@allontheboard

Service information

FOR A LOVER

LOVE WILL REMEMBER THE SUMMERTIME SADNESS,
AND ALL THE PERFECT PLACES WE GO
YOU'RE THE WIND BENEATH MY WINGS AND
                        WITH YOUR LUCKY HALO,
YOU SHINE YA LIGHT ON THE FEAR I KNOW.
IT'S A GOOD JOB LOVE DON'T COST A THING,
I BELIEVE THE BEST THINGS IN LIFE ARE FREE;
ALL I WANNA DO IS BE SOMEONE LIKE YOU,
YOU ARE MY HERO AND MY FANTASY.
IF CELEBRITY SKIN IS TORN AND BLEEDING LOVE,
OR THE RAIN IS FALLIN' ON YOUR UMBRELLA;
YOU SHAKE IT OFF AND LET IT GO,
                        WHEN LIFE IS COMPLICATED,
SO, THANK YOU FOR BEING SO STELLAR.
YOUR HIPS DON'T LIE AND WITH MY LITTLE EYE,
YOU'RE STILL THE ONE AND I FANCY YOU;
I WOULD FIGHT FOR THIS LOVE AND WHEN
                        I'M THINKING OF YOU,
I'M SIDE TO SIDE WITH THE THINGS YOU DO.

@allontheboard

Service information

Date HAPPY

Time VALENTINE'S DAY

FROM THE MOMENT I FIRST SAW YOU,

          I KNEW I WOULD ADORE YOU,

YOU'RE MY LOVER, YOU'RE MY SOULMATE AND MY BEST FRIEND;

MY HEART IS YOURS, SO KEEP IT, I TRUST YOU

                        WITH EVERY SECRET,

I CAN BE MYSELF WITH YOU AND NOT PRETEND.

YOU'RE SO STYLISH AND SO GOOD-LOOKING,

     GORDON RAMSAY COULDN'T COMPETE WITH YOUR COOKING,

I LOVE CHILLING WITH YOU WATCHING TV IN OUR PYJAMAS;

SOMETIMES WE DON'T SEE EYE TO EYE,

               BUT, YOU STILL GIVE ME BUTTERFLIES,

WHEN WE'RE SIDE BY SIDE WE CAN GET THROUGH ANY DRAMAS.

YOU MAKE ME FEEL BETTER WHEN I'M IN PAIN,

    YOU GIVE ME SHELTER AS WE 'DANCE THROUGH THE RAIN',

WHEN MY HEAD IS LIKE SPAGHETTI YOU HELP ME

                  UNRAVEL THE MUDDLE;

IF OUR WORLD IS A POD THEN WE ARE THE PEAS,

        YOU'RE IN ALL OF MY FAVOURITE MEMORIES,

WHEN WE'RE TOGETHER I LOVE A CHEEKY KISS AND A CUDDLE.

EVEN THOUGH WE SOMETIMES ARGUE,

         IT DOESN'T MEAN THAT I DON'T LOVE YOU,

I ALWAYS TRY MY BEST TO UNDERSTAND;

I WANT TO CHEER YOU UP WHEN YOU FEEL BLUE,

        HELP YOU MAKE YOUR DREAMS COME TRUE,

I'M SO PROUD TO BE THE ONE TO HOLD YOUR HAND.

@allontheboard

Service information

HOLD ME TIGHT

AT THE MOMENT,
    I NEED SOMEONE TO HOLD ME TIGHT,
TO CALM ME DOWN AND SAY, "IT'S ALRIGHT";
WHEN MY MIND IS IN DARKNESS,
    TO SWITCH ON THE LIGHT;
TO SHELTER ME FROM THE STORM AND
    KEEP ME WARM AT NIGHT;
TO BE THE WIND IN MY SAIL AND
    ALLOW ME TO SOAR LIKE A KITE;
TO BE MY SAFETY NET,
    IF I SHOULD FALL FROM A HEIGHT;
TO ADD COLOURS TO MY WORLD,
    WHEN THINGS ARE BLACK AND WHITE;
TO STAND BY MY SIDE WITH PRIDE AND
    HELP ME FIGHT;
BUT, AT THE MOMENT,
    I NEED SOMEONE TO HOLD ME TIGHT.

@allontheboard

Service information

IN THE END,
LOVE IS ALL THAT MATTERS;
IT MAY SOUND SIMPLE,
BUT, IT'S TRUE.
IF I COULD ONLY CHOOSE
THREE WORDS TO SAY,
FOR ETERNITY;
THEY WOULD SIMPLY BE,
        "I LOVE YOU".

@allontheboard

Service information

Date
Time

I want to be the reason you feel safe
and loved,
I want to be the reason why your heart
skips a beat;
I want to be the reason behind the butterflies
in your stomach,
I want to be the reason why you think your life is sweet.
I want to be the reason behind your smile,
I want to be the reason for the twinkle in your eye;
My words may sometimes be misunderstood,
but, every time you feel good,
I want to be the reason why.

@allontheboard

Love

 Service information

Date
Time

If I had a time machine
There's one thing I would do;
I would travel back
to the last time
We were together,
Hold you in my arms and say
how much I love you.

@allontheboard

83

Service information

If You Should Ever...

IF YOU SHOULD EVER FEEL DOWN,
I WILL BE YOUR CLOWN;
IF YOU SHOULD EVER FALL,
PLEASE GIVE ME A CALL;
IF YOU SHOULD EVER WORRY,
I WILL BE THERE IN A HURRY;
IF YOU SHOULD EVER CRY,
I WILL DRY YOUR EYES;
IF YOU SHOULD EVER GRIEVE,
I WILL BE THERE, PLEASE BELIEVE;
IF YOU SHOULD EVER BE IN A STATE,
I WILL HELP YOU TO CARRY THAT WEIGHT;
IF YOU SHOULD EVER FEEL ALONE,
I WILL BE YOUR COMFORT ZONE;
IF YOU SHOULD EVER NEED TO TALK,
I WILL LISTEN, AS WE GO FOR A WALK;
IF YOU SHOULD EVER BE IN PAIN,
I WILL GIVE YOU SHELTER FROM THE RAIN.

@allontheboard

Service information

Date

Time

JUST BECAUSE YOU'RE NOT
WITH ANYONE AT THE MOMENT,
DOESN'T MEAN YOU'RE NOT
          EASY TO LOVE;
LOVE COMES ALONG WHEN YOU
          LEAST EXPECT IT,
LIKE A SHOOTING STAR
IN THE NIGHT SKIES ABOVE.

@allontheboard

Service information

Date
Time VALENTINES DAY : ALTERNATIVES

GALENTINE'S DAY - SPEND IT WITH THE GIRLS

MALENTINE'S DAY - SPEND IT WITH THE LADS

PALENTINE'S DAY - SPEND IT WITH FRIENDS

SALENTINE'S DAY - SPEND IT SHOPPING

SAILENTINE'S DAY - SPEND IT ON A BOAT

RAILENTINE'S DAY - SPEND IT ON A TRAIN

NAILENTINE'S DAY - SPEND IT DOING D.I.Y

WAILENTINE'S DAY - SPEND IT AT THE KARAOKE

TALENTINE'S DAY - SPEND IT READING A BOOK

TAILENTINE'S DAY - SPEND IT WITH PETS

JAILENTINE'S DAY - AVOID THIS ONE

@allontheboard

Service information

Date *Michelle*

Time *& Barack*

by @allontheboard

THEIR FIRST DATE IN 1989 STARTED OFF WITH LUNCH
AT THE ART INSTITUTE OF CHICAGO,
AND ENDED UP WITH THE MOVIE 'DO THE RIGHT THING';
IN 1991 BARACK HAD JUST PASSED HIS BAR EXAM, THEY GOT ENGAGED OVER DINNER,
MICHELLE SAID YES WHEN THE WAITER CAME OVER WITH THE DESSERT AND A RING.
IN 1992 AFTER THREE YEARS OF DATING AND WAITING
THEY GOT MARRIED AND BECAME HUSBAND AND WIFE;
AT THE WEDDING BARACK DIDN'T PLEDGE ANY RICHES TO MICHELLE,
BUT, HE KEPT HIS PROMISE FOR THEM TO HAVE AN INTERESTING LIFE.
WHEN THEY SHARED ICE CREAM AT BASKIN-ROBBINS,
BOTH THEIR YOUNG HEARTS WERE THROBBING,
THEY WERE HOOKED UP BY THE LAW OF LOVE AND THEIR HARVARD CONNECTION;
A NEW ADVENTURE BEGAN FOR THEM WHEN THEIR BEAUTIFUL DAUGHTERS
WERE BORN,
THEY MOVED INTO THE WHITE HOUSE AFTER THEY WON THE PRESIDENTIAL ELECTION.
SO MANY MAGICAL MEMORIES FROM A WONDERFUL AMERICAN FAMILY,
SOME THINGS IN LIFE WERE TRULY MEANT TO BE;
MICHELLE AND BARACK ARE A COUPLE AS STRONG AS MARGE AND HOMER,
AND JUST AS COOL AS BEYONCÉ AND JAY Z.
THANKS SO MUCH TO THE OBAMAS FOR BEING TRULY INSPIRATIONAL,
IN TERMS OF GIVING TO THE WORLD THEY HAVE GIVEN PLENTY
THE EVIDENCE IS EVIDENT
ON THE WAY TO BECOMING MICHELLE OBAMA AND
ONE OF THE MOST ADMIRED WOMEN ON EARTH,
WE BELIEVE SHE WOULD BE AN AWESOME PRESIDENT.

@allontheboard

Service information

You're not perfect,
And neither am I ;
But, we are perfect
         for each other,
That's no word of a lie .

One of us may
         steal the covers,
And the other one
         may snore;
But, our 'perfect
         imperfections,'
Make us
     Love each other more.
          @allontheboard

Service information

Pets love you
Unconditionally
And never talk about you
Behind your back;
Pets are loyal,
They won't put you down
Or tell you what you lack.
Pets lessen loneliness
And give you purpose every day;
Pets keep you company,
They make you smile and play.
Pets help to reduce stress
And are good for sanity,
Pets can teach the human race
So much about humanity.

@allontheboard

Service information

'WHY HAVEN'T YOU
       GOT A PARTNER?',

'WHEN ARE YOU
       GETTING MARRIED?',

'ARE YOU GOING TO
       HAVE CHILDREN?',

Honestly,
Why do people need to know?;
Some questions people ask
  can silently hurt the recipient,
Just ask, 'How are you?'
And let the conversation flow.

@allontheboard

Service information

Date
Time

At the time I couldn't see
  through the tears,
My heart was broken and
  I felt blue.
But, now I know
  every failed relationship
  was a stepping stone.
And each one thankfully
  led me to you.

@allontheboard

Service information

Date THANK YOU FOR

Time BEING MY FRIEND

I am here for you and when I can I will prove it,
If there's something in the way, I will help you move it;
You truly make this Earth and my world a better place,
Your jokes make me laugh and I smile when I see your face.
I can tell you my secrets, we have shared
                                many memories over the years
I know you've got my back and would
                                try to dry my tears;
We may sometimes argue, but we make up in the end,
I'm sharing this board just to say,
                Thank YOU for being MY friend.

@allontheboard

Service information

When life gets dark
for someone
you care for,
Be the star
in their sky above.
When someone knows
you're not perfect
But, treats you
as if you are,
It really is true love.

@allontheboard

4

Always Remembered

Quite often we have been at work when news has broken of something terrible that has happened, and we have always tried to pay tribute or give our condolences by writing on a board about how we feel and sending our thoughts and love to those affected. Life moves on and the world still turns, but we must never forget the tragedies that have happened and the people who have lost their lives because of them.

The only thing that's guaranteed in life is death. We never know what will happen to us in our lives, what we will be and what we will do. All we know is that life is a journey and it does eventually come to an end. It always has and it always will. Death is as natural as birth, and yet it's a subject that many don't like talking about, and some fear.

When a loved one passes away, it's heart breaking and we all grieve in different ways. Losing a pet is equally devastating because they become family members, too.

In grief, we think we may never smile, enjoy life or laugh again, but there does come a day when we do. Sometimes our loved ones come to visit us to say hello in our dreams.

I send my love to all of my family, friends and pets up in heaven. I know I will see you again one day in the future. Until that day arrives, you will be forever loved and always remembered.

I was working at Warren Street station during the terror attacks on London in 2005 and it was a scary time of confusion and uncertainty for everyone living in this city.

It does seem like whenever there are tragic events that could potentially pull us apart we come together with resilience.

Whenever I write poems or messages I speak from my heart and try to put into words how I'm feeling and hopefully that resonates with other people possibly feeling the same. It's a poetic way of paying tribute to those who have passed away or been affected by tragedy and terrible events.

Loved ones who have passed on to the next life sometimes send us little reminders that they are still around, whether it be white feathers falling on the living room floor from nowhere, butterflies following you about, the whistling blackbird in the garden, certain songs coming on the radio and many other ways of remembering them.

The poems, quotes and messages we write are our way of saying 'we will always remember'.

There are many things in life we forget: such as where we left our keys or where the last bottle of milk went. It's impossible to hold on to every single thought, but we are unique creatures capable of holding on to the memories of the events and people that have impacted our lives the most, even if we cannot explain why. Those feelings stay with us forever, changing who we are and how we see the world, and steering us through some of our most difficult times.

It's vital to recognise the importance of our history, and the lessons it offers us. To embrace our emotional connection to moments and people is a part of being human, and the loss of a loved one is one of the most important yet difficult experiences a person will ever go through.

I remember how I've felt at the death of every loved one and every dear pet I've ever known, including the loss of my best friend when I was just 12 years old. Those moments stay with me, but I recall more strongly the many times we shared when they were alive, and the impact they had on me as a whole.

Those beautiful positives I cherish. They are a huge part of who

I am as a creative person, and I share them within these poems and everything I try to create.

Of course not all memories that impact us are positive, and yet the power of such negative events can be just as deep. I will never forget the King's Cross Fire in 1987, Grenfell Tower, and the many terrorist atrocities and natural disasters in London and across the globe that I have lived through. These events are catastrophic and those of us away from the event immediately connect our empathy as human beings with the victims, and the seen and unseen trauma of their loved ones. We can ask ourselves to consider what these moments mean to the lives of others, and how we would feel in their shoes.

When events like these unfold, N1 and I feel the need to express ourselves, and to help find a way to heal or support those in turmoil. We know it will be an exceptional moment, though for the wrong reasons, and that is why it's so important to respond swiftly. Loss that comes with those moments is extreme, hard to accept and confusing, and we hope that us writing about them can help ease the pain and remind everyone of where we can go from here. It is hard to remember that even our darkest days will end, and they do so with memories of a better past and visions of a brighter future. Devastating news has a deep impact on us all. You never forget where you were or what you were doing when you first heard of a tragedy or the death of somebody important to you.

Service information

Date
Time
REMEMBERING 7/7

LET THE LOVE INSIDE US, GUIDE US,
LET OUR DIFFERENCES NOT DIVIDE US;
ABIDE WITH EACH OTHER, TAKE PRIDE IN ONE ANOTHER,
ON THIS EARTH, WE SHOULD BE SISTERS AND BROTHERS.
AS THE WORLD KEEPS SPINNING, THINK FOR ONE SECOND,
HOW BEAUTIFUL THE HUMAN RACE IS;
WHAT'S THE POINT OF FIGHTING, HATE, WAR OR VIOLENCE,
OR LIVING LIFE WITH PREJUDICE?
THE THINGS WE BELIEVE IN, SHOULD NOT LEAVE US GRIEVING,
BUT, SHOULD TEACH US TO RESPECT ONE ANOTHER;
OUR LIVES ARE A JOURNEY THAT HAVE THE SAME ENDING,
AND STARTS IN THE WOMB OF A MOTHER.
SILENCE THE VIOLENCE, BUT, KILL HATE WITH LOVE,
BE OPEN, BE HOPEFUL AND TRUE;
WE CAN MAKE THIS WORLD BETTER, ONE STEP AT A TIME,
IF WE KEEP FAITH IN ME AND IN YOU.
FOR THOSE YOU LOVE, DON'T WALK AWAY,
BUT, WALK BESIDE THEM EVERY DAY;
FIND SOME STRENGTH AND COURAGE TAKE,
LOVE EACH OTHER, FOR THEIR SAKE.

@allontheboard

Service information

Date THE
Time AUSTRALIAN
BUSHFIRES

WE ARE THINKING OF OUR AUSSIE FRIENDS
DURING THIS TERRIBLE SITUATION,
HEARTBROKEN BY THE HUMAN AND ANIMAL LIVES LOST
AND THE DEVASTATION,
WE LOVE YOU AUSTRALIA
YOU ARE SUCH A BEAUTIFUL NATION.

@allontheboard

Service information

Racism is a reality
That we need to root out,
It's up to all of us
To not let others do it alone;
Even if some of us
Can't fully understand
How it truly feels,
We can listen and learn
From people whose lives are
Different from some of our own.
As human beings
None of us can look away
Or try to normalise the pain,
Silence can be louder than violence
In everything that we do;
Nobody has more right to be
On this earth than anybody else,
BLACK LIVES MATTER
Please know we stand by you.

@allontheboard

Service information

Date

Time **Caroline Flack**
1979 - 2020

As the sun sets on an island of love,
You will shine on forever in a paradise above;
Nobody will forget you, your personality,
         your walk and your infectious laugh,
Your departure has left so many hearts
                            broken in half.
May your ocean be calm, may there be no storm,
For eternity may you be happy
         and the light forever keep you warm,
May Heaven be as beautiful as you,
May you find true peace of mind,
There is no solution for our confusion,
 But, we need to always be kind.

@allontheboard

Service information

Date

Time

A MOTHER IS STILL A MOTHER AND A FATHER IS STILL
A FATHER EVEN IF THEY HAVE A CHILD IN HEAVEN
AND ARE NOT IN THIS WORLD TOGETHER;
THERE MAY BE YEARS OF MEMORIES OR THE
                              TIME MAY BE BRIEF,
BUT, IT DOESN'T DIMINISH THE LOVE OR THE GRIEF,
UNTIL PARENTS ARE REUNITED WITH THEIR CHILDREN
THEY WILL CARRY THEM INSIDE THEIR HEARTS FOREVER.

@allontheboard

Service information

To the people of
Christchurch,
New Zealand,
Our hearts break
with you
And we don't know
what to say;
For every life lost
and affected
You are in our thoughts
and we pray,
Terror has no religion,
no gender or race,
We just want it to go away.

@allontheboard

Service information

Date FOR
Time LOVED ONES
IN HEAVEN

TIME IS
    JUST A DISTANCE,
        THAT
    KEEPS OUR SOULS
            APART;
UNTIL THE DAY
    WE MEET AGAIN
YOU WILL BE
        FOREVER
IN MY HEART.

@allontheboard

Service information

Date

Time STOP BULLYING

by @allontheboard

IF YOU EVER FEEL LIKE YOU'RE BEING BULLIED
AT SCHOOL, COLLEGE, UNIVERSITY, WORK, IN LIFE
OR ONLINE;
THERE COMES A TIME WHEN ENOUGH IS ENOUGH
AND A POINT WHERE TO DRAW THE LINE.
TELL A FRIEND, TELL A TEACHER, TELL A FAMILY MEMBER
OR A COLLEAGUE,
THERE ARE ALSO ORGANISATIONS YOU CAN TRUST;
BULLIES ARE LIKE WASPS AND MOSQUITOES,
SO AGGRESSIVE AND ANNOYING,
IF IT COMES TO IT, THEN REPORTING THEM IS A MUST.
TRY TO IGNORE THEM, IT'S NOT YOU WITH THE PROBLEM,
EVEN THOUGH IT'S NOT EASY TO DO;
RAIN ON THEIR PARADE, DON'T FIGHT FIRE WITH FIRE,
BECAUSE THEY WANT A NEGATIVE REACTION FROM YOU.
THERE IS ALWAYS A REASON WHY A BULLY IS A BULLY,
FROM BAD PARENTING TO LOW SELF-ESTEEM;
THEY WILL EVENTUALLY LOSE A GRIP OF THEIR POWER TRIP
AND YOU WILL RISE TO THE TOP LIKE THE CREAM.

@allontheboard

Service information

We must
stand united against
hatred, prejudice
and intolerance.

Humanity owes it
to each victim that
it never happens again.
We cannot change
history, but history
can change us.
We must never forget.

@allontheboard

Service information

Date GRENFELL
Time TOWER

GRENFELL TOWER WASN'T JUST A BUILDING ON THE NEWS
ENGULFED IN FLAMES;
THE PEOPLE ARE NOT JUST STATISTICS, THEY ALL HAD LIVES AND NAMES.
IT WAS HEARTBREAKING WATCHING HELPLESSLY
AS THE FIRE RAGED AND THE SMOKE FILLED THE WEST LONDON SKY;
THE PAIN IN THE VOICES AND THE EYES
OF THE SURVIVORS AND THE RESIDENTS
AFFECTED US ALL
AND MADE THE WORLD CRY.

TO THE PEOPLE WHO DIED AND THE PEOPLE WHO SURVIVED
WE WILL NEVER FORGET THAT TRAGIC NIGHT
AND WE ARE THINKING OF YOU,
IF ONLY WOUNDS COULD HEAL FAST
AND AGONY COULD BE EASED WITH THE KIND WORDS SPOKEN;
AS BUILDINGS ACROSS LONDON ARE LIT UP GREEN,
WE HOPE THE SOLIDARITY AND SUPPORT CAN BE SEEN,
THROUGH THE STRUGGLES MAY YOU FIND STRENGTH
KNOWING YOUR COMMUNITY SPIRIT WILL NEVER BE BROKEN.

@allontheboard

Service information

Date 18TH NOVEMBER 1987
Time 19:30 HRS

REMEMBERING KING'S CROSS

ON THE 18TH OF NOVEMBER, WE SHALL STOP TO REMEMBER,
WHAT HAPPENED AT KING'S CROSS ALL THOSE YEARS AGO ON
THAT TRAGIC DAY;
EVEN THOUGH TIME IS A HEALER,
THEY SHALL ALWAYS BE MISSED
AND THE LOVE NEVER GOES AWAY.
REST IN PEACE TO THE VICTIMS,
THOUGHTS AND PRAYERS TO THEIR LOVED ONES,
MAY THE INJURED BE NO LONGER IN PAIN;
ALTHOUGH TIME KEEPS YOU APART,
MAY THEY REMAIN IN YOUR HEARTS,
UNTIL YOU MEET ONCE AGAIN.

Service information

Date
Time LITTLE ANGELS

A POEM FOR ANYONE WHO HAS LOST A CHILD
BY @allontheboard

A PERSON IS A PERSON, NO MATTER HOW SMALL,
SOMETIMES THE SMALLEST THINGS
        TAKE UP THE MOST ROOM IN YOUR HEART;
EVEN THOSE THAT NEVER BLOSSOM
        STILL BRING BEAUTY TO THIS WORLD,
GRIEF AND LOVE CAN BE AS TIMELESS AS A WORK OF ART.

EVERY NEW LIFE CHANGES THE WORLD FOREVER,
        IT DOESN'T MATTER HOW BRIEF,
THOSE WE HAVE HELD IN OUR ARMS FOR A SHORT TIME,
        WE WILL HOLD IN OUR HEARTS FOREVER
THERE'S NO FOOT SO SMALL THAT CAN'T LEAVE AN IMPRINT
        ON THIS EARTH;
A MEMORY MAY LAST LONGER THAN LIFE,
        UNTIL TIME BRINGS US BACK TOGETHER.

@allontheboard

Service information
Date
Time

Some mothers and fathers are not on this earth,
but, they keep a watchful eye over us from paradise;
When we are reunited in the future
They will continue to be our parents in heaven above.
Until that beautiful day when we see them again
Their legacies will live on in memories, lessons,
smiles, and stories,
We feel blessed for them blessing us with their
presence and love.

@allontheboard

Service information

Date 11th September 2001

Time

<u>FOR NEW YORK</u>

FOR OUR FRIENDS AND FAMILY IN NEW YORK,
WE ARE THINKING OF YOU ALL TODAY;
FROM ONE CITY TO ANOTHER,
WE ARE ONLY AN OCEAN AWAY.
THE EVENTS OF 9/11 WILL NEVER BE FORGOTTEN,
EVERY LIFE LOST WE SHALL ALWAYS REMEMBER;
OUR LOVE AND PRAYERS ARE WITH EVERYONE AFFECTED,
BY THAT TERRIBLE DAY IN SEPTEMBER.
FROM BROOKLYN, QUEENS, MANHATTAN
                    THE BRONX AND STATEN ISLAND,
TO CENTRAL PARK, TIMES SQUARE AND EMPIRE STATE;
MAY LADY LIBERTY SHINE HER TORCH, SO BRIGHTLY,
                    FOR OUR FREEDOM,
IT'S THE PEOPLE OF NEW YORK THAT MAKE IT GREAT.

@allontheboard

Service information

Date ONE LOVE
Time <u>MANCHESTER</u>

by @allontheboard

MANCHESTER IS A CITY UNITED
          BY THE RED HALF AND THE BLUE,
MAY A SKY FULL OF STARS SHINE FOR ETERNITY
      AND HOLD HANDS OF LOVE FOR THE TWENTY TWO.

LOVE IS EVERYTHING IF WE STAND UP FOR FREEDOM,
TOGETHER SIDE BY SIDE;
MAY YOU FIND THE STRENGTH TO BE MOVING MOUNTAINS,
THERE IS NO LIMIT TO MANCUNIAN PRIDE.

ALL AROUND THE WORLD WE SHALL JUST PRAY,
AND IF WE COULD WE WOULD FIX YOU WITH LOVE;
WE WILL NEVER FORGET THE TWENTY TWO ANGELS,
SO, PUT YOUR HEARTS UP TO HEAVEN ABOVE.

WE ARE THINKING OF YOU, IF YOU THINK 'WHERE IS THE LOVE?',
IT WILL BE RIGHT HERE UNCONDITIONALLY;
DON'T FORGET WHERE YOU BELONG, DON'T LET GO AND CARRY ON,
WITH THE STRENGTH OF A MANCHESTER BEE.

IN OUR MINDS, IN OUR DREAMS AND IN OUR HEARTS,
THE TWENTY TWO ANGELS SHALL LIVE FOREVER;
TIME IS A DISTANCE THAT KEEPS US APART,
AND IN TIME WE SHALL ALL BE TOGETHER.

@allontheboard

Service information

If people say "it's just a pet"
they really don't understand,
The presence of a pet
can change our hearts forever;
They become family
from the moment they
                enter our lives,
We share memories to treasure
            and adventures together.
Pets give us friendship
that nobody else could;
They are our sidekicks
        and they keep us company;
Our hearts truly get broken
    when they pass away and
            we have to say goodbye,
But, we will love them
@allontheboard   for eternity.

Service information

Date _PUT THE_
Time _KNIVES DOWN_

by @allontheboard

BY TAKING SOMEONE'S LIFE WHAT DOES ANYONE ACHIEVE?,
ONE FAMILY LEFT DEVASTATED, WHILE ANOTHER FAMILY GRIEVE;
ON THESE STREETS WE ARE NOT SOLDIERS,
KILLING EACH OTHER FOR PRIDE OR A POSTCODE DOESN'T MAKE SENSE,
IF WE STOP, THINK AND DON'T ATTACK,

THERE'S NO NEED FOR A DEFENCE.
THERE IS NO PROBLEM THAT CAN'T BE SOLVED BY

TALKING OR WALKING AWAY,
DON'T CARRY A KNIFE TO END A LIFE,
IT'S SENSELESS AND POINTLESS AT THE END OF THE DAY;
YEARS SPENT IN PRISON FOR A FOOLISH DECISION

THAT DESTROYS SO MANY LIVES,
DON'T BE A STATISTIC OR A PART OF THE PROBLEM,
THINK FOR YOURSELVES AND PUT DOWN THE KNIVES.

Service information

Date USA

Time SHOOTINGS

Our thoughts and prayers are truly with you
On yet another tragic day,
from Daytona, Ohio to El Paso, Texas
and our friends in the USA;
Santa Fe we are here for you,
Please know we are only half a world away;
Yesterday was already too late, this can't go on,
We are with you all the way.
Las Vegas we are thinking of you,
May the bright lights of your city shine forever;
It's hard to find the right words to say for what
                    happened at Mandalay Bay
May you find the strength to carry on and stand together.
Let the stars at night shine big and bright
            in the darkness of the prairie sky;
deep in the heart of Texas and Sutherland Springs
May you catch one another's tears that you cry.
Florida you will always be the Sunshine State,
Even when the sun doesn't shine up above;
No words can be spoken to fix hearts that are
                    broken across the ocean.
From London and the United Kingdom we are sending our love.

@allontheboard

Service information

Date

Time

WE ARE LONDON AND SHALL NOT FALL,
WITH DEFIANCE WE WILL DEFEAT THE VIOLENCE
AND TRIUMPHANTLY STAND TALL;
IF YOU WISH TO COPY EVIL
IF YOUR AIM IS TO SPREAD FEAR ,
IF HATE IS IN YOUR VISION
YOU SHOULD SEE YOU ARE NOT WANTED HERE.
TERROR MAY SHAKE US BUT IT WON'T BREAK US
IF WE ARE SIDE BY SIDE;
IF WE'RE THERE FOR EACH OTHER WE CAN
CONQUER THE FEAR WITH COURAGE AND PRIDE
LET RELIGIONS NOT DIVIDE US OR THE COLOUR OF OUR SKIN;
KEEP FAITH IN ONE ANOTHER, WE ARE HUMANS
MADE THE SAME WAY AND LOVE WILL ALWAYS WIN.
AN ATTACK ON ANY ONE OF US
IS AN ATTACK ON US ALL,
HATERS ARE NOT WELCOME
WE ARE LONDON AND SHALL NOT FALL.

@allontheboard

Service information

Date WE SHALL

Time <u>REMEMBER</u>...

WE SHALL REMEMBER THEIR COURAGE,
AS THEY FOUGHT THROUGH THE CARNAGE
AND EACH SACRIFICE THEY MADE,
WE SHALL REMEMBER THEIR BRAVERY
AND THE BLOOD THAT WAS SHED
AND THE ULTIMATE PRICE THAT THEY PAID
WE SHALL REMEMBER EACH SOLDIER
          FROM ALL OVER THE WORLD,
BY WEARING A POPPY AND WITH EACH
          WREATH WE LAY;
WE SHALL REMEMBER THE FALLEN
          AND THOSE WHO RETURNED
DURING THE SILENCE ON REMEMBRANCE DAY

          @allontheboard

5

Random Treasures

&

SIMPLE Pleasures

Hmmmmm . . . what are your simple pleasures?

Think of all the things that you like doing or experiencing that bring you joy and are simple. Here are some of the small things that I enjoy, that just seem to make life a whole lot better for me.

If I have a pen and a piece of paper to write poems, stories or songs, I am happy. I love getting lost inside my mind to see what spills out on to the paper. Sometimes it's good, sometimes it's bad, but it's always something that I've created. Creating is an absolute joy.

Simple hugs are fantastic, especially with friends and family. They make you feel safe and forget about the troubles in the world. Beds are amazing too – a comfortable bed that welcomes you home and is hard to leave is very special. If I ever got to travel back in time, I would give the inventor of the bed a massive hug.

Watching clouds float by high up in the sky is a favourite pastime for me, and trying to make animal shapes out of them. In fact, any shape made from clouds will do. And the sound of the rain on a window pane makes me happy. Actually, I love the sound of rain on anything. The heavier it falls, the more I seem to enjoy it.

My favourite food is quite possibly ice cream. I could eat it all day and I've never met a flavour that I didn't like, but I do have a particular weakness for bubble-gum-flavoured ice cream with rainbow sprinkles and strawberry sauce. The sound of an ice cream van's chimes can fill a heart with joy as you hurry down the road to where it is parked.

It's also a great feeling when you make someone smile. A genuine kind of smile. Maybe you've done something that has made them happy, or given a gift that was wanted, or passed on some good news or a daft joke. It's brilliant when you make a baby smile. You make funny noises or pull faces, and when they eventually smile you feel like you have achieved something amazing. It's such a good feeling. It's a pleasure. And simple. A simple pleasure.

These pleasures make my life so much better, but my favourite has to be spending time with my family and friends. Even if we are going nowhere and doing nothing, there is no other place that I would rather be. I feel blessed in their presence.

In this chapter you will find some things we (and probably many others) enjoy. As individual as we all are, we do have so much in common. Maybe you will see some of the things you treasure here.

We don't just write about the complicated and difficult things in life, we also write about the simple ones: tea, beds, pizza, fashion – the things that make us happy in between everything else. We write silly things, and love using wordplay to do that. Life is about the little things, and their impact on who we are.

I wouldn't be me without stories. Then again, would anyone? I love all forms of storytelling, but movies are by far my favourite. They are a huge part of my life and I love watching and making them. N1 and I have ideas we would love to film one day.

Family and friends is another one. To many they will seem like ordinary pleasures, and they are in that they are not something particularly epic, like a bungee jump or flying a helicopter on your day off. Being with family and friends, though, certainly makes me feel as good as the most epic of activities, and they ask for nothing in return but for me to be there with them. I love my family and would do anything for them.

I love drawing, too. When I was young I wanted to be an artist, and in some ways I am. I paint when I can or draw on our boards when the poem warrants it.

Tea is the first thing I consider when it comes to taking a short moment out of the world, and my taste has changed over the years. I drink green tea now, but ten years ago I would have struggled with that. As we get older we change and our tastes and preferences change with us, as do other things such as our sense of humour.

All On The Board's humour is almost always random, something we do when we feel the urge to share what we think will make others smile. It could be the renaming of a station or the twisting of a song lyric or title to mean something entirely different and hilarious (Elton John's 'Rocketman', anyone?). We include some here, and we plan to write many more in the future. We certainly hope you get our sense of humour as you read this chapter.

When in London I often look up to see the wonderous pieces of architecture that go unseen to many and I don't mean the big recognisable icons. Try it, there are quirks in all parts of London that are somewhat hidden gems. It's a lovely way to break through the hustle and bustle and it is both a simple pleasure and a random treasure because you never know what you might see. I have no doubt this is the same in all cities around the globe, and if it's not the buildings that bring you joy, your eyes will stumble on the beauty of the skies above.

Service information

Date

Time

ELTON JOHN IS....

ROCKETMAN

HE WON'T GO BREAKING YOUR
HEART AND KNOWS SATURDAY
NIGHT IS ALRIGHT FOR FIGHTING...
.... CRIME.

Random Treasures & Simple Pleasures

 Service information

EMOJIS ARE GREAT,
THEY ARE MODERN DAY
      HIEROGLYPHICS,
YOU CAN PUT A

 OR

IF YOU DON'T FEEL TERRIFIC;
THEY ARE NOT

SO, DON'T GET SCIENTIFIC.

Service information

A FRUIT & VEG

GUIDE TO LIFE

Don't be <u>BANANAS</u>,
Give <u>PEAS</u> a chance,
We can <u>TURNIP</u> around;
<u>BEETROOT</u> to ourselves,
It doesn't matter where we've <u>BEAN</u>,
From a tree or grown in the ground.
<u>LETTUCE</u> not fear,
<u>OLIVE</u> in a world of Greed,
There's so <u>MUSHROOM</u> to spare;
Wouldn't it be <u>GRAPE</u>,
To put our differences aside,
<u>RAISIN</u> love and hope to live like a <u>PEAR</u>.

@allontheboard

Service information

Date **Winnie the Pooh**

Time (Inspired by quotes from Winnie the Pooh and his friends) @allontheboard

DON'T UNDERESTIMATE THE VALUE OF DOING NOTHING AND JUST GETTING ALONG,

PEOPLE SAY NOTHING IS IMPOSSIBLE, BUT I DO NOTHING EVERYDAY;

A LITTLE CONSIDERATION AND A LITTLE THOUGHT FOR OTHERS CAN MAKE ALL THE DIFFERENCE,

IT NEVER HURTS TO KEEP LOOKING FOR SUNSHINE ANYWAY.

NOBODY CAN BE UNCHEERED WITH A BALLOON,

IF THE STRING BREAKS, THEN WE TRY ANOTHER PIECE OF STRING;

A DAY WITHOUT A FRIEND IS LIKE A POT WITHOUT A SINGLE DROP OF HONEY LEFT INSIDE,

PLEASE DON'T BE UPSET, I DIDN'T FORGET, I JUST WASN'T REMEMBERING.

THE THINGS THAT MAKE ME DIFFERENT ARE THE THINGS THAT MAKE ME, ME,

A HUG IS ALWAYS THE RIGHT SIZE,

BUT, SOMETIMES THE SMALLEST THINGS TAKE UP THE MOST ROOM IN A HEART;

I ALWAYS GET TO WHERE I'M GOING BY WALKING AWAY FROM WHERE I'VE BEEN,

I'M BRAVER THAN I BELIEVE, STRONGER THAN I SEEM AND I CAN BE SMART.

HOW LUCKY AM I TO HAVE SOMETHING THAT MAKES SAYING GOODBYE SO HARD,

BUT, OH BOTHER, THERE MAY COME A DAY WHEN WE CAN'T BE TOGETHER;

IF WE'RE IN EACH OTHER'S DREAMS WE CAN BE TOGETHER ALL THE TIME,

PROMISE YOU WON'T FORGET ME EVER, KEEP ME IN YOUR HEART AND I'LL STAY THERE FOREVER.

ANY DAY SPENT WITH YOU IS MY FAVOURITE DAY,

WHEN I'M RUMBLY IN MY TUMBLY, I'M NEVER AFRAID WITH YOU;

SOME PEOPLE CARE TOO MUCH, I THINK IT'S CALLED LOVE,

IF WE'RE NOT THERE ALREADY, THERE'S NO HURRY, WE SHALL GET THERE SOMEDAY TOO.

@allontheboard

Service information

HUGS ARE A BEAUTIFUL
FORM OF COMMUNICATION,
FOR ANY SITUATION,

THEY ARE A SILENT WAY
OF SAYING YOU MATTER,
WITH NO WORDS TO SAY;

IF I'M GRIEVING
I NEED TO RECEIVE THEM
TO BELIEVE
I'M NOT ALONE,
THEY MAY NOT HAVE
THE ANSWER, BUT,
THEY MAKE US FEEL
BETTER WHEN WE
@allontheboard HAVE A BAD DAY.

Service information

Date
Time **FASHION**

FASHIONS FADE, STYLE IS ETERNAL,
CLOTHES REFLECT AN ERA, IT'S TRUE;
FASHION IS ALL ABOUT HAPPINESS, IT'S NOT A MEDICINE OR A CURE,
WHEN IN DOUBT WEAR RED, IF YOU'RE FEELING BLUE.
DELETE THE NEGATIVE, ACCENTUATE THE POSITIVE,
THERE ARE HINTS ABOUT WHO YOU ARE IN WHAT YOU WEAR;
BELIEVE IN YOURSELF AND BE PREPARED TO WORK HARD,
BE COMFORTABLE IN YOUR CLOTHES AND SHOW THE WORLD YOU CARE.
HOW PEOPLE DRESS ON THEIR DAYS OFF CAN BE INTRIGUING,
BE INSPIRED BY THE GIRL ON THE STREET OR THE MAN ABOUT TOWN;
BE DARING, BE DIFFERENT, BE IMPRACTICAL,
BE ABSOLUTELY FABULOUS AND NEVER LOOK DOWN.
IMPERFECTIONS CAN BE MORE BEAUTIFUL AND MORE INTERESTING,
AND FASHION IS THE REASON FOR GOING SOME PLACES;
ELEGANCE IS A QUESTION OF PERSONALITY AND EXCESS IS SUCCESS,
WITH A PASSION TO BRING SMILES TO FACES.
FASHION DOESN'T HAVE TO BE ABOUT LABELS OR BRANDS,
IT'S SOMETHING ELSE THAT COMES FROM INSIDE;
YOU CAN FIND INSPIRATION IN EVERYTHING,
IF YOU WEAR YOUR HEART ON YOUR SLEEVE WITH PRIDE.

@allontheboard

Service information

MY BED
IS AN ISLAND

by
@allontheboard

I LOVE MY BED,
MY BED LOVES ME;
MY BED IS AN ISLAND,
THE FLOOR IS THE SEA.
THE PILLOW IS A CLOUD,
WHERE I REST MY HEAD;
THE DUVET IS A MOUNTAIN,
THAT'S SOFTER THAN BREAD.
IT'S ALWAYS SPRING ON MY ISLAND,
WHATEVER THE WEATHER;
WE HAVE THE SAME DREAMS,
AND SHARE ADVENTURES TOGETHER.
BISCUIT CRUMBS ON THE SHEETS,
ARE JUST TINY ROCKS,
THE FISH THAT SWIM BY,
ARE MAINLY PANTS, BRAS AND SOCKS.
THE MATTRESS IS THE LAND,
A PARADISE OF FOAM;
MY BED IS AN ISLAND,
THAT ALWAYS WELCOMES ME HOME.

@allontheboard

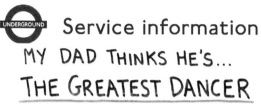

Service information

MY DAD THINKS HE'S...
THE GREATEST DANCER

by @allontheboard

MY DAD THINKS HE'S
            THE GREATEST DANCER,
HE WON'T HAVE IT ANY OTHER WAY;
HE COMPARES HIMSELF TO JOHN TRAVOLTA
            IN 'SATURDAY NIGHT FEVER'
BUT, HE DANCES LIKE THERESA MAY.
MY DAD THINKS HE'S
            THE GREATEST DANCER,
WHEN HE GYRATES IT LOOKS QUITE OBSCENE;
HE REALLY NEEDS TO WORK
            ON HIS FLOSS AND TWERK,
HE THRUSTS HIS PELVIS LIKE MR BEAN.
MY DAD THINKS HE'S
            THE GREATEST DANCER,
HE'S THE FIRST ON THE FLOOR
            AT EVERY PARTY AND WEDDING;
MUM TOLD HIM TO QUIT,
            WHEN HE ATTEMPTED THE SPLITS,
HE DID HIS BACK IN AND IT DID HER HEAD IN.
@allontheboard

Service information

PIRATE TALK

by @allontheboard

IT DOESN'T MATTER IF YOUR PIRATE ATTIRE IS NOT UP
TO SCRATCH,
YOU DON'T NEED TO OWN A PARROT OR WEAR AN EYE PATCH;
YOU DON'T NEED A JOLLY ROGER WITH A SKULL AND CROSSBONES,
AS A SCREENSAVER ON YOUR LAPTOP OR WALLPAPER ON
YOUR PHONES.
YOU DON'T NEED TO HAVE GOLD BARS OR PIECES OF EIGHT
IN THE BANK,
YOU DON'T NEED TO GET SICK SAILING SEAS OR EVER
WALK THE PLANK;
YOU DON'T NEED A JOHNNY DEPP SWAGGER,
WITH A CAPTAIN JACK WALK,
JUST BATTEN DOWN THE HATCHES AND PREPARE YOUR
PIRATE TALK.

YOU MAY BE A LANDLUBBER,
BUT, THERE'S NO NEED FOR LIMBERS,
TO SAY 'YO HO HO', 'ALL HANDS AHOY'
OR 'BLIMEY! SHIVER ME TIMBERS';
BUT, IF YOU DO TAKE A TRIP ON A PIRATE SHIP,
KEEP A GRIP OR THE WET DECK MAY MAKE YOU SLIP.

@allontheboard

Service information

Date
Time **Pizza Poem**

By @allontheboard

TODAY IS THE DAY,
TO GRAB A PIZZA THE ACTION;
TAKE IT EASY, GET CHEESY
AND TOP IT WITH SATISFACTION.
BE A FUNGI WITH MUSHROOMS,
UPON A BASE THAT'S DEEP PAN;
IF YOU MUST, STUFF YOUR CRUST
AND SHARE A NICE SLICE OF THE PLAN.
A MARGHERITA SENORITA,
MET A MOZZARELLA FELLA;
THE DATE WAS GREAT AND WITH A KISS,
HE THEN WHISPERED, 'CIAO BELLA'.
IS IT FINER IN A DINER,
OR FROM A DELIVERY?
WE ALL 'DOUGH' THE BEST THING
                    SINCE SLICED BREAD,
COMES FROM ITALY.

@allontheboard

Service information

Eating popcorn is groovy.
While watching a movie,
It's the essential snack
for a cinema and theatre crowd;
But, during quiet moments
                  of the film,
Popcorn can sound ever so loud.

Service information

Date SESAME STREET

Time   INSPIRED BY
CHARACTER'S QUOTES

by @allontheboard

SESAME STREET IS A PLACE WHERE PEOPLE, BIRDS,
                MUPPETS AND MONSTERS ALL LIVE IN HARMONY,
BUT, YOU'D BE A GRUMPY GROUCH TOO, IF YOU LIVED IN A TRASH CAN;
BAD DAYS HAPPEN TO EVERYONE, BUT, WHEN ONE HAPPENS TO YOU
                DON'T FEEL BAD ABOUT YOURSELF,
JUST KEEP DOING YOUR BEST WHEN THINGS DON'T GO TO PLAN.
FRIEND SOMETHING BETTER THAN CHOCOLATE ICE CREAM,
MAYBE FRIEND SOMEBODY YOU GIVE UP LAST COOKIE FOR;
LIFE'S LIKE A MOVIE, SO WRITE YOUR OWN ENDING,
IF YOU DREAM OF MAKING PEOPLE HAPPY BY SINGING AND DANCING,
                DO IT SOME MORE.
SOME DAYS I THINK I LOOK CUTE AND OTHER DAYS
                I TRY TO AVOID THE MIRROR,
IF LIFE IS FAIR WHY DOES EVERY ROSE HAVE A THORN;
WISE SAYINGS OFTEN FALL ON BARREN GROUND,
                BUT, A KIND WORD IS NEVER THROWN AWAY,
IT'S GOOD TO BE ALIVE AND TO BE GLAD OF BEING BORN.
TRY TO BE OPTIMISTIC LIKE ELMO,
        VALUE FRIENDSHIP LIKE BERT AND ERNIE,
            BE CARING LIKE BIG BIRD, GROVER AND ABBY,
                HELP YOUR FRIENDS WITH THEIR FEARS;
THANK YOU SESAME STREET FOR ENTERTAINING US
                AND TEACHING US LIFE'S LESSONS
YOU HAVE WELCOMED US TO YOUR NEIGHBOURHOOD FOR
        SO MANY YEARS.

@allontheboard

Service information

THERE'S NOT ENOUGH HOURS IN THE DAY. I DON'T KNOW WHAT TO DO WITH MY TIME. I HATE BEING COLD. I DON'T LIKE IT TOO HOT. I'VE GOT OVER 200 CHANNELS ON MY TV, BUT, THERE'S NOTHING FOR ME TO WATCH. I DON'T LIKE SINGING THE BLUES.......

RED WHINE

Service information

Date

Time **STORYTELLING**

STORYTELLING ISN'T JUST FOR A CHILD'S BEDTIME,
WE TELL STORIES EVERY DAY OF OUR LIVES;
POLITICIANS TO VOTERS, PATIENTS TO DENTISTS, EMPLOYEES TO BOSSES
AND HUSBANDS TO WIVES.
WE GO TO THE CINEMA TO WATCH STORIES ON THE SILVER SCREEN,
LADS TELL STORIES TO EACH OTHER IN A PUB;
STORIES CAN BE TOLD BY LOOKS, DON'T JUDGE THE COVER OF A BOOK,
WE DANCE TO STORIES SUNG BY SINGERS IN A CLUB.
A PRINCESS OR THE BOY IN THE DRESS MAY HAVE TO KISS A TOAD,
TO FIND A LITTLE PRINCE OR A GRUFFALO,
THEN SHE CAN WRITE IT IN A DIARY, LIKE BRIDGET JONES;
THE HUNGER GAMES ARE TRAGIC, HARRY POTTER IS MAGIC,
AND IN THE TWILIGHT YOU MIGHT FEEL ALRIGHT WITH LOVELY BONES.
THE BOOK THIEF HAS WHITE TEETH AND LIVES ON BRICK LANE,
HE HAS MORE BLING THAN CHRISTIAN GREY AND THE LORD OF THE RINGS
THE GIRL WHO PLAYED WITH FIRE SUNG A BIRDSONG SLIGHTLY HIGHER,
AND CAN KILL MOCKING BIRDS WHEN SHE SINGS.
STORIES ARE TOLD ON SOCIAL MEDIA WITH PHOTOS AND SELFIES,
FROM NURSERY RHYMES TO REMINISCING WHEN WE'RE OLD;
I REMEMBER TELLING A TEACHER THAT MY DOG ATE MY HOMEWORK,
THROUGHOUT OUR LIVES THERE WILL BE STORIES FOREVER TOLD.

@allontheboard

Service information

THE BEAUTY OF TEA

PUT THE KETTLE ON AND MAKE A CUPPA,
IT'S THE PERFECT LIFTER UPPER;
DO YOU RISK IT WITH YOUR BISCUITS AND DUNK THEM
FAR TOO LONG?
DO YOU PREFER YOUR TEA WITH SUGAR?
DO YOU LIKE IT WEAK OR STRONG?
A NICE BREW CAN MAKE THINGS BETTER
AND CAN ALSO QUENCH YOUR THIRST,
ARE YOU ONE OF THOSE WHO PUT THE MILK IN FIRST?
A CUP OF TEA CAN COMFORT YOU IN ANY SITUATION,
THEY ARE GREAT TO DRINK WITH SOMEONE WHEN
YOU'RE SHARING PROBLEMS AND GOSSIP
OR HAVING A HEARTFELT CONVERSATION.

@allontheboard

Service information

Date
Time

TOAST

HERE'S A TOAST,
TO THE FOOD WE LOVE THE MOST;
THE BEST THING SINCE SLICED BREAD,
ALSO KNOWN AS TOAST.
IT'S EXCITING WAITING FOR IT,
TO POP OUT OF THE TOASTER;
IT DOESN'T MAKE YOU NAUSEOUS
LIKE A ROLLERCOASTER.
YOU CAN HAVE IT WITH JAM LIKE BOB MARLEY,
OR A PEANUT BUTTER SPREAD;
YOU CAN EAT IT ON THE MOVE,
OR A CHEEKY SLICE IN BED.
IT GOES WELL WITH MELTED CHEESE,
OR A SAUCY CUP OF TEA;
OR MAKE IT INTO SOLDIERS
LIKE MUM USED TO DO FOR ME.

@allontheboard

ALL ON THE BOARD

 ## Service information

Date

Time

IF YOU'RE ZONED OUT
IN A WORLD OF YOUR OWN
OR YOU'RE BUSY
DEVISING A PLAN;
THERE IS NOTHING
THAT CAN SNAP YOU
        OUT OF IT
OR GRAB YOUR
        ATTENTION,
QUITE LIKE
    THE CHIMES OF AN ICE CREAM VAN.

@allontheboard

142

Service information

I LOVE SLEEP,
FROM CHEEKY POWER NAPS
  TO THE ONES THAT ARE DEEP;
HERE'S A LITTLE SHOUT OUT
              TO MY BLANKET,
IT KEEPS ME COSY AND
              I WANT TO THANK IT;
I LOVE CATCHING Z'S
              AND FORTY WINKS,
IF I'M TIRED AND EXPIRED
  AND MY MIND IS ON THE BLINK;
THERE'S NOTHING QUITE LIKE
        AN UNDISTURBED SLUMBER,
BETWEEN SIX AND EIGHT HOURS
              IS A MAGIC NUMBER;
IN THE LAND OF NOD
    I MAY DREAM AND SNORE,
WHEN I WAKE UP I COULD
    SLEEP FOR A FEW HOURS MORE.

@allontheboard

6

Mental Health

I used to be a train driver on the London Underground and once, while I was driving a train, a young girl jumped out in front of it. Just before the train hit her, everything seemed to go in slow motion, our eyes met and then she smiled. As the train struck her, time sped up again. It felt as if I was living out a scene in a movie and having an out-of-body experience at the same time. Afterwards, I would have anxiety attacks, and I experienced bouts of depression, hallucinations, flashbacks of the incident, and vivid nightmares replaying the situation. I would often see the girl's face in my mind, and when I did she was always smiling. Counsellors would tell me that the girl was smiling to tell me that it's alright, but my mind turned it into an evil, twisted smile. Like the Joker from *Batman*.

My mental health was telling me that my career as a train driver was over and I moved on to work at the stations instead. I still have bad days sometimes, but I'm able to deal with the stress much better because I can talk to people when I'm feeling anxious. When I was driving a train, I was on my own and unable to talk to anybody.

Anxiety attacks or panic attacks – whatever you call them – can cause the scariest sensations in the world. Unless you have actually experienced one, you could never know how terrifying they can be. The main symptoms I experience are a pounding heart, and my throat feels tight as if I can't breathe or swallow. I get aches and pains in my muscles, my knees feel weak and my mind starts racing, visualising all kinds of worst-case scenarios. I feel an overwhelming feeling of impending doom and paranoia, and in that moment I believe I am dying.

Mental distractions work for me: talking to people, playing games that challenge my mind, breathing techniques and writing. When I feel anxious, I like to be creative by writing poetry (trying to make words rhyme with as many words as possible). Writing short stories, or even just noting down my feelings or the sensations I'm experiencing and what I'm thinking while I'm having a panic attack seem to work for me.

Different distraction techniques succeed for different people, and you will eventually find a technique that works for you. We – EI and myself – often come across people having anxiety attacks at Tube stations, and we use these techniques to help people. We are certainly not experts in any kind of mental health capacity, but we are two humans who will listen.

Sometimes the loneliest place you can be is inside your own head. It can be so hard to reach out for help, but there is help out there. Whatever mental health issues you or a loved one have, you are not alone. Remember that millions of people feel the same way too.

Eating disorders are considered a serious mental health condition. As a man, I know full well that we do not talk about them much, if at all. They are largely, and wrongly, considered unique to females, and are usually about controlling our lives when other things aren't going well. I hardly talk about what I went through when I lived with one throughout my teenage years, and how it has impacted my entire life. I learnt how to manage it, like all my conditions, which took many years.

Many men with eating disorders keep it a secret and this is perhaps the most dangerous thing of all. Not recognising a problem exists, or trying to keep it from others, damages so many aspects of our lives and keeps us from truly living.

I look back and wonder if my eating disorder led to most of my other conditions, and I am increasingly convinced that it was key. With help sooner, my conditions could have been less damaging, and that is why it is so important to talk and share, and get help.

I am not an expert, I simply write what I feel from my experience, but with N1 I have found that our voices seem to echo those of many others who feel and live through the same experiences, even those with seemingly unrelated conditions. Perhaps these feelings are where many health concerns begin and thrive, and if we can work together to raise awareness, we can support people emotionally in ways that science can't.

This chapter is a collection of poems and quotes about mental health, some of the conditions we have, and others we want to raise awareness of. We hope you find something that echoes your voice, experiences or struggles, as well as sheds light on illnesses you'd like to better understand.

We all have good days and bad days, ups and downs and it's hard. There is no 'one size fits all' solution but supporting, talking and being there for each other will help. Sometimes all it takes is a reminder that this moment will end and a better one is on the horizon. Just getting through that moment is what matters.

One of the really special things that has come from All On The Board is our amazing online community. Often a person who is having a tough time will comment under our boards posted online and the way others respond is truly beautiful. It is so special to read. People recognise the plight of another human being and want to help or support. I have had to engage with people who were in a dark moment but in the dangerous environment of a station platform. Never underestimate the power of talking to someone if you feel something is not right. You could make someone's day or even save a life.

Service information

Date DON'T DELETE

Time YOURSELF

DON'T DELETE YOURSELF
        FROM THE WORLD,
IF YOU FEEL YOU HAVE
        REACHED YOUR LIMIT;
THERE ARE PEOPLE YOU CAN
        TALK TO WHO WILL HELP
SHOW YOU BEAUTY IN LIFE
AND HOW MUCH BETTER IT IS
        WITH YOU IN IT.

@allontheboard

UNDERGROUND Service information

A POEM FOR NO ONE

INSPIRED BY **THE BEATLES**

I TRY TO ACT NATURALLY, WHEN I'M COPING WITH MY MISERY,
I'M LIKE THE FOOL ON THE HILL WHO ALWAYS JUST PRETENDS;
EVERY LITTLE THING IS GREAT, BUT,
I NEED HELP TO CARRY THAT WEIGHT,
I KNOW I'LL BE BACK,
WITH A LITTLE HELP FROM MY FRIENDS.

LIFE CAN BE A MAGICAL MYSTERY TOUR, WHEN
I WALK THE LONG AND WINDING ROAD,
MY BRAIN IS A HELTER SKELTER AND
I NEED SHELTER FROM THE RAIN
TOMORROW NEVER KNOWS, BUT,
THERE'S A PLACE WHERE REAL LOVE GROWS,
TO SHAKE OFF THESE CHAINS AND BE AS
FREE AS A BIRD ONCE AGAIN.

HERE, THERE AND EVERYWHERE,
ACROSS THE UNIVERSE,
FROM THE INNER LIGHT TO WHAT GOES ON
IN THE SPACE ABOVE;
I'M FIXING A HOLE INSIDE MY SOUL,
KNOWING WE CAN WORK IT OUT
BECAUSE IN THE END ALL YOU NEED IS LOVE.

@allontheboard

Service information

'Are you Okay?'

It could mean
        the world to someone,
And it only takes
            two seconds to say;
If you start a conversation,
By asking, 'Are you Okay?'
They could be your lover,
        your sister or brother,
A family member,
    a colleague or a friend;
We can be there for each other,
        We need one another,
We are all the same in the end.

@allontheboard

Service information

Date

Time

THERE WILL ALWAYS BE
A BETTER DAY;
THERE WILL ALWAYS BE
ANOTHER WAY.

Service information

Date

Time

BIPOLAR
DISORDER

By @allontheboard

SOMETIMES ITS HARD TO KEEP CALM WHEN YOU'RE ON AN EMOTIONAL ROLLERCOASTER,
AND TERRIFIED THE RIDE WILL NEVER STOP,
SO QUICKLY THE MOOD SWINGS VICIOUSLY FROM FEELING ELATED TO DEFLATED,
ANXIOUSLY LOOKING OVER THE EDGE WHEN YOU REACH THE TOP
FROM DOWNWARD SPIRALS TO UPWARD SMILES, SELF-LOATHING TO UNREALISTIC BELIEFS,
BIPOLAR DISORDER IS NOT A TREND, A BUZZ WORD OR A FASHION,
THE MOOD CHANGES ARE SO INTENSE IT CAN AFFECT THE ABILITY TO FUNCTION,
ITS A MENTAL ILLNESS WHICH REQUIRES UNDERSTANDING AND COMPASSION.
FROM PERIODS OF FEELING UP AND ENERGISED
               TO FEELING DOWN, EXHAUSTED AND TRAUMATISED,
THE HIGHS OF MANIA AND LOWS OF DEPRESSION CAN MESS WITH THE HEAD;
EPISODES CAN SEVERELY AFFECT RELATIONSHIPS, WORK AND ALL ASPECTS OF EVERYDAY LIFE,
THE MOOD CHANGES ARE DRAINING AND MAKE IT HARD TO GET OUT OF BED.
IT CAN LEAVE YOU FEELING HOPELESS, SAD AND EMPTY, UNABLE TO EXPERIENCE PLEASURE,
IRRITABLE, WORTHLESS, GUILTY AND SLUGGISH FROM FATIGUE,
ONE MOMENT THOUGHTS ARE RACING ALL OVER THE PLACE, ITS HARD TO CONCENTRATE,
THEN THE MOOD CAN SHIFT SUDDENLY AND LEAVE YOU AT THE BOTTOM OF THE LEAGUE.
LEARNING AS MUCH AS YOU CAN, WILL HELP ASSIST WITH YOUR RECOVERY,
EXERCISE CAN ALSO BE BENEFICIAL TO YOUR MOOD,
CARING SUPPORTIVE PEOPLE CAN HELP CALM THE NERVOUS SYSTEM
TRY TO GET ENOUGH SLEEP AND ALSO EAT HEALTHY FOOD.
AVOID EXTREMELY STRESSFUL SITUATIONS,
               MAINTAIN A HEALTHY WORK-LIFE BALANCE,
TRY TO DISCOVER A SUITABLE RELAXATION TECHNIQUE,
GET MEDICAL HELP, GET THE RIGHT MEDICATION, JOIN A SUPPORT GROUP
               AND TALK TO A TRUSTED FRIEND,
REACHING OUT FOR HELP IS NOT A SIGN OF BEING WEAK.

@allontheboard

Service information

Date

Time **BODY IMAGE**

WHEN I LOOK INTO THE MIRROR SOMETIMES I DON'T LIKE
WHAT'S LOOKING BACK,

MY EYES DON'T ALWAYS RECOGNISE THE PERSON WHO I SEE;
IN A ROOM FULL OF PEOPLE I WANT TO BE SOMEONE ELSE,
I WISH I COULD LEARN TO LOVE MYSELF,
INSTEAD OF CRYING IN BED WISHING I WASN'T ME.
STEP AWAY FROM THE MIRROR AND LOOK FOR YOUR REFLECTION
IN SOMEONE'S EYES,

SELF-ESTEEM DOESN'T COME FROM ANY BODY PARTS;
WE HAVE MORE TO OFFER THE WORLD THAN OUR BODIES AND APPEARANCE
EXPERIENCE KNOWS TRUE BEAUTY COMES FROM KINDNESS, MINDS
AND HEARTS.

YOU WERE BORN THIS WAY, TO BE REAL NOT TO BE PERFECT,
BE BRAVE, BE BRUISED, BE WHO YOU'RE MEANT TO BE;
TREAT YOUR BODY LIKE IT BELONGS TO SOMEONE YOU LOVE,
EMBRACE WHO YOU ARE BECAUSE NOBODY'S PERFECT,

WHEN YOU LOOK INTO THE MIRROR PLEASE BE PROUD OF WHO YOU SEE.
NEVER SACRIFICE YOUR MENTAL HEALTH TO HAVE A 'PERFECT BODY',
EVERYTHING YOU ARE IS MORE THAN GOOD ENOUGH;
EVERY HUMAN BEING IS IMPERFECT, WE ARE NOT MADE
TO LOOK LIKE DOLLS,
PROUDLY SHOW OFF SCARS AS EVIDENCE THAT YOU SURVIVED
WHEN LIFE GOT TOUGH.

@allontheboard

Service information

Date
Time <u>CHILDREN'S MENTAL HEALTH</u>

By @allontheboard

CHILDREN GET SAD, CHILDREN FEEL BAD
CHILDREN SOMETIMES THINK THEY ARE GOING MAD;
CHILDREN GET STRESSED, CHILDREN GET DEPRESSED
CHILDREN SOMETIMES THINK THEIR LIVES ARE A MESS.

A CHILD'S MENTAL HEALTH IS MORE IMPORTANT
THAN ANY SCHOOL GRADE;
IT'S UP TO US TO GIVE THEM THE COURAGE
TO SPEAK UP AND NOT BE AFRAID.

@allontheboard

Service information

Date
Time

WHY CRY ALONE?

WHEN WE CAN DO IT TOGETHER,

SHOULDER TO SHOULDER,

WINGS WRAPPED AS ONE;

WHEN TWO PEOPLE HURT THE SAME,

THE TEARS MAY POUR LIKE RAIN,

BUT IT WONT BE LONG,

BEFORE WE CAN SEE THE SUN.

@allontheboard

Service information

Date

Time **DEPRESSION**

SOME DAYS ARE GOOD, SOME DAYS ARE BAD,
SOME BATTLES I WIN AND LOSE;
SOME DAYS I FEEL LIKE I'M ON THE RIGHT PATH,
OR EVERY STEP IS A MILE IN MY SHOES.
SOME DAYS I'M ENLIGHTENED, SOME DAYS I'M FRIGHTENED,
AND I SEEM TO QUESTION EVERY DECISION;
THERE ARE MOMENTS I FEEL AS FREE AS A BIRD,
AND AT TIMES MY MIND SEEMS LIKE A PRISON.

MY MOOD CHANGES LIKE THE WEATHER,
         I'M AS LIGHT AS A FEATHER,
AND THEN MY HEART IS A HEAVY STONE;
EVEN THOUGH I'M SOMETIMES LONELY,
              I'M NOT THE ONLY ONE
AND I KNOW THAT I'M NOT ALONE.
                              @allontheboard

Service information

DON'T STOP

IF YOU FEEL YOUR FACE DOESN'T FIT,
AND YOU FEEL FIT TO DROP;
YOU MAY BE FLIPPING OUT,
BECAUSE YOU FEEL LIKE A FLOP;
DON'T BE HARD ON YOURSELF,
YOU ARE TOP OF THE POPS;
IT TAKES A BIT OF PRACTICE,
TO GET STICKS TO CHOP.
IT'S NOT FUNNY FOR A BUNNY,
IF THEY DON'T KNOW HOW TO HOP;
OR IF YOU HAVEN'T GOT THE MONEY,
TO BUY SOME HONEY FROM A SHOP;
IF LIFE STARTS TO WIPE THE FLOOR WITH YOU,
AND TREATS YOU LIKE A MOP;
BE YOURSELF BECAUSE YOU'RE WORTH IT,
AND IT'S SAFE TO SAY 'DON'T STOP'.

@allontheboard

Service information

Date

Time **EATING DISORDERS**

AN EATING DISORDER IS A MENTAL ILLNESS, IT'S NOT A LIFESTYLE CHOICE,
YOU ARE BEING EATEN ALIVE BY YOUR FEELINGS, EMOTIONS AND
THOUGHTS IN A PAINFUL SITUATION;
EVERYBODY NEEDS HELP FOR RECOVERY, IT CAN BE SO TOUGH FOR
YOU, YOUR FRIENDS AND FAMILY,
BUT, TOGETHER WE CAN BEAT IT WITH THE RIGHT SUPPORT
AND MORE INFORMATION.

IF YOU ACCEPT WHO YOU ARE AND LEARN TO LOVE YOURSELF,
THEN YOU WILL SEE YOUR REFLECTION CHANGE;
THE STRUGGLE THAT YOU GO THROUGH IS PART OF THE PROCESS,
IF YOU RELAPSE DON'T THINK THAT YOU HAVE FAILED OR THAT
YOU'RE STRANGE.

CARE ABOUT YOURSELF AND YOU WILL EVENTUALLY OVERCOME
YOUR DEMONS,
EAT WITHOUT REGRET AND KNOW YOUR TRUE WORTH;
STOP COMPARING YOURSELF TO A FALSE PERFECTION IN SOME PHOTOS
IN MAGAZINES OR ONLINE,
SURROUND YOURSELF WITH THE BEAUTIFUL TRUTH UPON THIS EARTH.

GET YOUR FEELINGS OUT, DON'T INFLICT SELF-HARM UPON YOUR BODY,
DON'T JUDGE SOMEBODY ELSE AND SEE IMAGE AS A COMPETITION;
IT'S NOT ENOUGH TO JUST SURVIVE, EVERYBODY WITH A HEART SHOULD
START TO FEEL ALIVE,
BY GETTING HELP AND TREATMENT FOR YOUR MEDICAL CONDITION.

@allontheboard

Service information

Date

Time ___ GET HELP ___

SOMETIMES IT'S HARD TO FUNCTION BEING RIDDLED WITH FEAR,

IF I COULD DO MAGIC I WOULD CHOOSE TO DISAPPEAR;

MY HEAD FEELS SO FUZZY AND MY VISION ISN'T CLEAR,

IF I SENT A POSTCARD I WOULDN'T WISH ANYONE HERE.

SADNESS, ANGER AND FRUSTRATION OFTEN PRODUCE A TEAR,

I DON'T RECOGNISE MY REFLECTION OR THE THINGS I HOLD DEAR;

TODAY ISN'T MINE, IT DOESN'T FEEL LIKE MY YEAR,

IT'S TIME TO GET HELP AND FIND A LISTENING EAR.

YOU ARE NOT ALONE.
THERE ARE PEOPLE AND
ORGANISATIONS WHO WILL
LISTEN AND HELP YOU,
NO MATTER WHERE YOU
ARE IN THIS WORLD.

@allontheboard

Service information

Date

Time

IF SOMEONE ASKS 'ARE YOU ALRIGHT?'

BUT, YOU FEEL HALF LEFT TODAY;

IT'S QUITE ALRIGHT TO NOT FEEL RIGHT

AND OKAY NOT TO BE OKAY.

@allontheboard

Service information

Even though
You may not feel it,
Please believe it,
Because it's
        absolutely true;
You were
Important yesterday,
You are
Important today,
You will be
Important tomorrow too.

@allontheboard

Service information

INSIDE I FEEL

INSIDE I FEEL LIKE I'M BROKEN,
EVEN THOUGH YOU CAN'T
SEE A PLASTER CAST;
INSIDE I FEEL LESS EXCITED
ABOUT THE FUTURE,
EVEN THOUGH YOU CAN'T
SEE HOW I FELT IN THE PAST.
INSIDE I FEEL LIKE I'VE BEEN
BEATEN UP,
EVEN THOUGH YOU CAN'T
SEE ANY BRUISE;
INSIDE I FEEL EVERY DAY
IS A MARATHON,
EVEN THOUGH YOU CAN'T
SEE WORN OUT SHOES.

Service information

IT'S NOT JUST ME

WHEN PEOPLE LOOK AT ME, WHAT DO THEY SEE?
I FEEL ROOTED TO THE SPOT, JUST LIKE A TREE,
IS THIS WHERE I'M SUPPOSED TO BE?
I'M LACKING IN VITAMINS B, C AND D,
WHAT IS THE COST FOR BEING FREE?
SOMETIMES I FEEL LOST AT SEA,
DISCONNECTED FROM REALITY,
QUESTIONING MY SANITY,
FEELING GUILTY FOR MY JEALOUSY,
RELYING TOO MUCH ON FRIENDS AND FAMILY,
SOMETIMES I FEEL INVISIBLE WITH COMPANY,
ESCAPING FROM MY LIFE THROUGH A TV,
IN NEED OF SYMPATHY AND EMPATHY,
OR EARS TO LISTEN, WITH A CUP OF TEA,
WOULD MY MOOD BE IMPROVED WITH A SPENDING SPREE?
AM I FOLLOWING THE SCRIPT OF MY DESTINY? I FEEL I CAN'T
DEAL WITH DRAMA OR A TRAGEDY,
I KNOW OTHERS FEEL THE SAME, IT'S NOT JUST ME.

@allontheboard

Service information

Date
Time **OKAY TO NOT BE OKAY**

DON'T BE TOO HARD ON YOURSELF,
IT'S OKAY TO NOT BE OKAY;
FROM POPSTARS TO THE QUEEN,
AND STARS OF THE SILVER SCREEN,
EVERYONE ON EARTH
CAN HAVE A DIFFICULT DAY.

@allontheboard

Service information

Date

Time **MENTAL HEALTH**

IF YOU'RE FEELING SAD OR DOWN,
OR LIKE A STRANGER IN YOUR TOWN,
WITH A LOSS OF FOCUS AND LACKING CONCENTRATION;
YOU COULD BE FEELING SO CONFUSED
                          AND YOUR MIND MAY FEEL ABUSED,
BY RACING THOUGHTS OF WORRY AND FRUSTRATION.
YOU MAY HAVE FEELINGS OF GUILT AND WANT TO
                                    HIDE UNDER A QUILT,
THE CHANGES IN YOUR MOOD CAN BE EXTREME;
REALITY CAN SEEM FALSE, YOUR BODY AND SOUL
                                CAN FEEL DIVORCED,
AND YOU LOOK FOR WARNING SIGNS IN EVERY DREAM.
BECAUSE OF ANXIETIES YOU MAY WITHDRAW FROM ACTIVITIES,
WITH TROUBLE SLEEPING AND SOME PROBLEMS WHEN YOU EAT,
YOU MAY HAVE GIVEN UP HOPE OF AN ABILITY TO COPE,
AND EVERY TASK SEEMS TOO IMPOSSIBLE TO COMPLETE,
YOU MAY ALWAYS SECOND GUESS WHEN YOU'RE
                          DEALING WITH STRESS,
WHEN YOUR HEART IS HEAVY LIKE A STONE;
THROUGH ANY KIND OF WEATHER,
                    LET'S WALK AND TALK TOGETHER,
AND ALL OF US CAN KNOW WE ARE NOT ALONE.

@allontheboard

Service information

Date

Time

MODERN DAY LONELINESS

THERE DOESN'T SEEM TO BE ENOUGH HOURS IN THE DAY,
BITS AND PIECES TAKE UP TIME
AND MODERN LIFE GETS IN THE WAY;
IT CAN STILL FEEL LONELY WITH ACCESS TO MILLIONS OF
PEOPLE ON A SMART PHONE;
SOME OPEN UP A BOTTLE AND POUR A LIQUID COMPANION
INTO A GLASS,
CARRYING LONELINESS AROUND WITH THEM AND
QUESTIONING THE PAST,
FEELING GUILTY THAT THEY HAVE LOVED ONES AND
SO MUCH TO LOOK FORWARD TO,
BUT, THEY STILL FEEL ALONE.

WHY DO I FEEL LONELY? IS IT JUST ME?
IN THIS PRESENT DAY OF PUSHING BUTTONS AND SWIPING,
HOW IS IT POSSIBLE TO BE?
I STILL FEEL LONELY WHEN I'M SWAPPING STORIES WITH
FRIENDS OVER MEALS AND SHARING A BED;
PLANNING ADVENTURES, DOING HOUSEHOLD CHORES,
TRYING TO MANAGE A CHALLENGING WORK-LIFE BALANCE
AND PACING MANY FLOORS,
IF I KEEP BUSY CAN I KEEP THE SADNESS OF MODERN DAY
LONELINESS AWAY FROM MY HEAD?

Service information

Date

Time

WHATEVER MENTAL HEALTH ISSUES YOU
OR A LOVED ONE HAVE,
YOU ARE DEFINITELY NOT ALONE,

THE WEIGHT OF THE WORLD CAN BE
LESSENED EVERY TIME WE TALK AND SHARE;

SOMETIMES THE LONELIEST PLACE YOU CAN BE
IS INSIDE YOUR OWN HEAD,
IT CAN BE SO HARD TO REACH OUT FOR HELP,
BUT, THERE IS HELP OUT THERE.

@allontheboard

Service information

Date

Time **ONE DAY**

ONE DAY I FEEL HAPPY,
THE NEXT DAY I FEEL SAD;
ONE DAY I FEEL GOOD,
THE NEXT DAY I FEEL BAD.
ONE DAY I FEEL FULL OF ENERGY,
THE NEXT DAY I FEEL WORN OUT;
ONE DAY I FEEL CONFIDENT,
THE NEXT DAY I FEEL FULL OF DOUBT.
ONE DAY I FEEL CAREFREE,
THE NEXT DAY I FEEL I CARE TOO MUCH;
ONE DAY I FEEL ON TOP OF THINGS,
THE NEXT DAY I FEEL OUT OF TOUCH.
ONE DAY I FEEL BRAVE,
THE NEXT DAY I FEEL SCARED;
ONE DAY I FEEL READY,
THE NEXT DAY I FEEL UNPREPARED.
ONE DAY I FEEL PROUD
THE NEXT DAY I FEEL SHAME;
BUT, I SHOULD NEVER FEEL ALONE,
BECAUSE OTHER PEOPLE FEEL THE SAME.

@allontheboard

Service information

Date
Time ___PANIC ATTACKS___

PANIC ATTACKS CAN HAPPEN ANYWHERE,
THEY SIMPLY COME FROM OUT OF THE BLUE;
FROM LAYING IN BED TO WATCHING A MOVIE,
OR STANDING IN A QUEUE.
UNLESS SOMEONE HAS EXPERIENCED THEM,
THEY REALLY WOULDN'T UNDERSTAND;
HOW DEVASTATING AND FRUSTRATING THEY CAN BE,
AND LIFE CAN SEEM SO OUT OF HAND.
THEY MAKE YOU FEEL PARANOID AND SOUL DESTROYED,
WITH UNWANTED TRIPS TO A&E;
A CRACK IN THE PAVEMENT BECOMES A CAVERNOUS VOID,
AND THE LIGHT IS HARD TO SEE.
FIGHT OR FLIGHT CAN CAUSE A FRIGHT,
WHEN YOUR MIND PREPARES YOUR BODY FOR ACTION;
BUT, KNOWLEDGE IS POWER FOR DEFEATING THEM,
WITH EXERCISE, RELAXATION AND DISTRACTION.
TREAT A PANIC ATTACK LIKE AN UNINVITED GUEST,
OR SEE IT AS AN IRRITATING FRIEND;
IT CAUSES DISCOMFORT AND IS REALLY ANNOYING,
BUT, IT CAN'T HURT YOU AND SOON IT WILL END.

@allontheboard

UNDERGROUND ## Service information

Date

Time

If your brain
    feels scrambled
and no matter how
    hard you fry, Life isn't going
eggsactly as you planned and
    you feel like you're cracking,
Please don't fry to be hard boiled
    and withdraw into your shell,
Please talk to someone.
Life isn't always sunny side up
    and Mental Health is no yolk.

@allontheboard

UNDERGROUND # Service information

WHAT IF......

by
@allontheboard

WHAT IF I GO FOR A WALK,
AND CAN'T FIND MY WAY BACK?
WHAT IF I GO FOR A RUN,
AND HAVE A HEART ATTACK?
WHAT IF I HAVE TO SAY A SPEECH,
AND THEN FORGET MY WORDS?
WHAT IF I SIT UNDER TREES,
AND GET DECORATED BY SOME BIRDS?
WHAT IF I GO SHOPPING,
AND IN THE AISLE I COLLAPSE?
WHAT IF I MISS EVERY STEP,
WHEN I'M BUSY MINDING THE GAPS?
WHAT IF I TRY TO COMPETE,
AND THEN LOSE EVERY GAME?
WHAT IF EVERYONE I KNOW,
ALL FORGOT MY NAME?
WHAT IF I GO FOR A MEAL,
AND SUDDENLY I CHOKE?
WHAT IF I TRY TO BE FUNNY,
AND NOBODY GETS THE JOKE?
WHAT IF I GO TO THE DOCTORS,
AND THEY SAY I'M REALLY ILL?
WHAT IF I GET MOTION SICKNESS,
WHEN I'M TRYING TO BE STILL?
WHAT IF I GO TO THE DENTIST,
AND THEY REMOVE ALL MY TEETH?
WHAT IF I'M NOT STRONG ENOUGH
TO DEAL WITH SORROW OR GRIEF?
WHAT IF I STOP FIGHTING,
WITH THE DEMONS IN MY HEAD?
WHAT IF I COULD STOP WORRYING
AND LIVE MY LIFE INSTEAD?

We are all legends in our own way, and there are legends all around us.

If the person serving you ice cream adds an extra scoop or a dollop (I love that word) in your cone, in your bowl or on your plate for free, then they are a legend. If the person styling or cutting your hair makes it look particularly good, they are a legend too.

We say it all the time to people who have done us a favour, or given us something that we like or love: 'You're a legend for doing this,' or, 'You're a legend for being there.' Sometimes just, 'You're a ledge!!' (shout out to all of the window ledges out there too).

All On The Board has sometimes been called a legend too. Sometimes we have truly felt like legends, and other times we have felt more like LEG ENDS.

Without blowing our own trumpets – because we don't own trumpets and wouldn't know how to play them even if we did – at least some of the things we have created have been seen as legendary.

All we really intended to do was to try to put smiles on people's faces with a little creativity on the station boards. We could never have imagined what would happen next. We have gained so many wonderful followers, been shared by loads of celebrities who we admire and consider to be legends. We've been on TV and radio, appeared in newspapers and have become sort of infamous. And we also have our own book out too. All while doing our day jobs of being station assistants.

Is it legendary? Are we legendary? Are we legends?

Legends are seen in a positive way, people valued for doing something or saying something which has inspired or been appreciated by somebody else.

Here are some poems for people who are well-known and who we consider legends, who have inspired us personally with their music, their movies, their philosophies, their words, their achievements, their actions, their compassion and their creativity.

At some point you may have been called a legend yourself. Quite clearly YOU are a legend for having this book. Congratulations for being a legend, and thank you once again.

What makes a person a legend?

We all know someone who fits the bill. To me, N1 is a legend, and so are my loved ones. To most, the definition of a legend is to be well-known, but if that is true then how well-known is enough? Is there a single person that every living person on earth has heard of? Most definitely not. So, how many people need to know you before you qualify as a legend? Do you need to have accomplished something unique or impossible? Or, to be a legend, do you need to be worthy of immortality?

Once upon a time, legendary status was attained by word of mouth over a long period. Today you can reach it in an instant, thanks to social media. A previously unknown former British Army officer aged 99 years old became a legend in just a matter of days during the coronavirus pandemic. More about him later.

People often ask us why we write these poems about people they don't know, or who are not as famous as others. To be honest, there's no exact science to it. It's a feeling N1 and I share towards someone – we admire a certain person who we feel deserves the status for what they have achieved, or who they are. Some of their feats might seem small, but everyone has their own goals and achieving them is worth shouting about from the rooftops, whatever anyone else thinks. Often, others share our feelings about our legends, and it does bring us joy knowing we are not alone in thinking that person is a wonderful gem who is worth the time we spend writing about them. It's another positive thing we can all share.

Of course some of these legends are celebrities, but that is not to take away those from who are not. We all know someone who deserves to be considered: the doctor who has saved countless lives, the scientist who discovered a world-changing breakthrough, the janitor who lived through countless wars and atrocities, and influenced some of the most powerful people on earth. Or perhaps the local pub quiz genius? All are worthy of a legendary status if that's how you feel about them. Big Dave up the street is a legend, so is Sally from Southend. We know them, but you likely don't. They deserve a board too but we can't write a board about every individual, and some legends are better off in the hearts of those who know them best. I won't even try to guess how long it would take to write a board for everyone. We would probably need a few superpowers to do that but we shall certainly give it our best shot.

For now we've included a few legend poems we hope you enjoy. And if they make you smile, then they've been a worthy inclusion in many ways.

Service information

Date **Amy**
Time **Winehouse**

by
@allontheboard

EVERY CUPID KNOWS THAT TEARS DRY ON THEIR OWN,
AFTER SOME UNHOLY WAR OF WORDS
      WE MAY WAKE UP ALONE,
DURING HALF TIME BETWEEN THE CHEATS WE MAY THINK
      LOVE IS A LOSING GAME;
TAKE THE BOX OF HIDDEN TREASURES AWAY,
IT TAKES MORE THAN PUMPS AND FORBIDDEN PLEASURES
      TO IMPRESS A LIONESS TODAY,

VALERIE AND FRANK WERE JUST FRIENDS AND BOTH FELT THE SAME
ON THE ROULETTE WHEEL ME & MR. JONES WENT BACK TO BLACK,
OUR DAY WILL COME WHEN WE DON'T DISCUSS THE WEALTH WE LACK.
IF YOU'RE WONDERING NOW (THERE IS) NO GREATER LOVE
      THAN WHAT I FEEL FOR YOU;
SOMETIMES THIS LIFE FEELS STRONGER THAN ME,
AND IN MY BED IS THE ONLY PLACE THAT I WANT TO BE,
I HEARD LOVE IS BLIND, BUT, YOU SENT ME FLYING, IT'S TRUE
YOU KNOW I'M NO GOOD REMEMBERING TO RETURN WHAT I BORROW.
WITH YOUR BODY AND SOUL WILL YOU STILL LOVE ME TOMORROW?
IF I WRITE A SONG FOR YOU IN THE AUTUMN IT WILL BE
      AN OCTOBER SONG;
MAY YOU FIND YOUR SMILE IN A SOUL ASYLUM,
OR WHEN YOU HELP YOURSELF IN REHAB,
I'M ADDICTED TO THE COMFORTS OF THE ZONE WHERE I BELONG.

@allontheboard

UNDERGROUND Service information

Date **BRUCE**

Time **LEE**

(INSPIRED BY THE WORDS OF A LEGEND) By @allontheboard

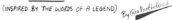

IF YOU LOVE LIFE, DON'T WASTE TIME, FOR TIME IS WHAT LIFE IS MADE UP OF,
IF YOU SPEND TOO MUCH TIME THINKING ABOUT A THING, YOU'LL NEVER GET IT DONE;
ABSORB WHAT IS USEFUL, DISCARD WHAT IS USELESS AND ADD WHAT IS SPECIFICALLY YOUR OWN,
DO NOT PRAY FOR AN EASY LIFE, PRAY FOR THE STRENGTH TO ENJOY A DIFFICULT ONE.

MISTAKES ARE ALWAYS FORGIVABLE, IF ONE HAS THE COURAGE TO ADMIT THEM,
KNOWING IS NOT ENOUGH, WE MUST APPLY AND BE WILLING TO DO;
THE KEY TO IMMORTALITY IS FIRST LIVING A LIFE WORTH REMEMBERING,
REAL LIVING IS LIVING FOR OTHERS AND OTHERS LIVING FOR YOU.

ALWAYS BE YOURSELF, EXPRESS YOURSELF AND HAVE FAITH IN YOURSELF,
DON'T TRY TO DUPLICATE SOMEBODY ELSE'S SUCCESSFUL PERSONALITY;
THE MEDICINE FOR SUFFERING IS WITHIN YOU FROM THE VERY BEGINNING,
IN THE MIDDLE OF CHAOS LIES OPPORTUNITY.

@allontheboard

Service information

Date

Time   DAVID BECKHAM

YOU HAVE ALWAYS HAD AN EYE FOR FASHION SINCE YOU WERE A KID,
MAKING FLAT CAPS LOOK COOL BEFORE THE PEAKY BLINDERS DID,
A GO GETTING TRENDSETTER WHO CAN MAKE SARONGS LOOK SO RIGHT;
FROM LEYTONSTONE TO LOS ANGELES THE WHOLE WORLD IS UNITED,
YOU ARE ONE OF ENGLAND'S GREATEST SONS AND
                    IT'S TIME THAT YOU GOT KNIGHTED,
EVEN THE CROWN JEWELS COULDN'T COMPETE WITH GOLDEN BALLS
                            SHINING SO BRIGHT.
SUPPLYING   THE CROSSES AGAINST BAYERN MUNICH
                        TO COMPLETE THE MONUMENTAL TREBLE,
YOU ARE A FOOTBALL GOD AND A TRUE RED DEVIL,
A LEGEND WITH HOLLYWOOD FILM STAR LOOKS AND TROPHIES GALORE;
EVEN URI GELLER COULD NEVER BEND IT LIKE YOU,
GRADUATING INTO GREATNESS WITH YOUR MATES FROM THE CLASS OF '92,
YOU'RE A FAMILY MAN WITH CHILDREN YOU CHERISH
                        AND A WIFE YOU ADORE.
AT MANCHESTER UNITED, PRESTON NORTH END AND REAL MADRID,
YOU ROSE TO EVERY CHALLENGE WITH THE COURAGE OF THREE LIONS
                            AND NEVER HID,
CREATING JOY AND MEMORIES AT PSG, AC MILAN AND L.A. GALAXY;
YOU MAKE HAIRSTYLES AND TATTOOS LOOK LIKE A WORK OF ART,
A GLOBAL ICON WHO LOVES PIE AND MASH,
                    WITH THE EAST END IN YOUR HEART,
WEARING YOUR HEART ON YOUR SLEEVE,
            IT DIDN'T MATTER IF YOU WERE 7, 32 OR 23.

@allontheboard

Service information

Date

Time

DAVID BOWIE by @allontheboard

BORN IN A UFO, THE MAN WHO FELL TO EARTH LANDED IN BRIXTON,
A LONELY PLANET OF DREAMS SAID `HALLO SPACEBOY`
AND WATCHED HIS BRILLIANT ADVENTURE OF TRANSCENDING
                              INTO THE STARMAN;
WE HOPE HE FELT SOUL LOVE FROM STATION TO STATION,
HE GAVE A MOONAGE DAYDREAM TO BELIEVE IN FOR EVERY GENERATION,
WITH A SPACE ODDITY TO FORGET THE SORROW OF REALITY
                    WHEN PEACE DOESN'T GO TO PLAN
AFTER ALL, TIME IS BORROWED. EVEN FOR LIFE ON MARS?
                        AFTER TODAY COMES TOMORROW,
AT 5:15 THE ANGELS HAVE GONE, BUT THERE'S NO NEED TO BE AFRAID;
THE MEMORIES OF THE GOLDEN YEARS WILL
                    RISE LIKE LAZARUS FROM ASHES TO ASHES,
IT'S IMPOSSIBLE FOR THE PRETTIEST STAR TO SLIP AWAY INTO THE SHADE
FROM DANCING IN THE STREET TO DANCING OUT IN SPACE
            LOOKING FOR SATELLITES ON A FANTASTIC VOYAGE,
IT'S A REAL COOL WORLD WHEN WE LEARN HOW TO FLY;
TIME WILL CRAWL AND YET CATCH UP WITH US ALL,
AS WE GET STUCK IN A LABYRINTH WONDERING `WHERE ARE WE NOW?`
THE BLACKSTAR SHINES ON FOREVER IN HEAVEN, UP IN THE SKY.

@allontheboard

Service information

Date FOR

Time <u>MARTIN LUTHER KING JR</u>
1929 - 1968

(INSPIRED BY HIS QUOTES)

WHATEVER YOU DO YOU HAVE TO
        KEEP MOVING FORWARD,
WITH THE TOUGHNESS OF THE SERPENT
        AND THE SOFTNESS OF THE DOVE;
THE TIME IS ALWAYS RIGHT
        TO DO WHAT IS RIGHT,
HATE IS TOO GREAT OF A BURDEN,
        WE SHOULD STICK WITH LOVE.
MARTIN LUTHER KING JR. IS INCOMPARABLE,
HE WILL ALWAYS BE ONE OF A KIND;
A SPIRIT WHO WILL INSPIRE FOR ETERNITY,
WITH A BEAUTIFUL DREAM
        AND A BEAUTIFUL MIND.

Service information

Date

Time **MICHAEL CAINE**

by @allontheboard

THE MAN WHO WOULD BE KING KNEW HE
WOULDN'T BE A KING OF THIEVES;
HE WAS PROUD OF THE PRESTIGE OF EDUCATING RITA
ON HOW TO HIDE ACES UP HER SLEEVES.
HANNAH AND HER SISTERS THOUGHT THAT
ALFIE WAS AN INTERSTELLAR FELLA,
HE NEVER PLAYED BY THE CIDER HOUSE RULES;
EVEN DIRTY ROTTEN SCOUNDRELS KNOW THAT TO
COMPLETE THE ITALIAN JOB,
THEY MIGHT NEED TO GET CARTER TO GET THEM THE RIGHT TOOLS.
WHEN BATMAN BEGINS TO SING AT THE KARAOKE
HIS LITTLE VOICE IS FULL OF SURPRISES;
EVERY TIME HIS NAME GETS CALLED OUT TO PERFORM
ALWAYS THE DARK KNIGHT RISES.
THE DARK KNIGHT OUT ON THE TOWN WITH HARRY BROWN
ENDS UP GOING IN STYLE;
THE QUIET AMERICAN WAS A SLEUTH WITHOUT A CLUE
WHEN IT CAME TO EXAMINING THE IPCRESS FILE.
THE EAGLE HAS LANDED ON A BEACH OUT OF REACH,
BLAME IT ON RIO FOR BEING A BRIDGE TOO FAR;
THE MUPPET CHRISTMAS CAROL WAS ENDED TOO SOON
WHEN THEY SAW SECOND HAND LIONS RUSH
FOR LAST ORDERS AT THE BAR.
MICHAEL CAINE IS AN ICONIC BERMONDSEY BOY AND
FROM ROTHERHITHE TO HOLLYWOOD,
HE'S LOVED BY EVERY AGE AND ALL OF THE CLASSES;
HE'S A LEGENDARY SOUTH LONDONER AND
NOBODY HAS EVER LOOKED AS COOL WHEN WEARING GLASSES.

Service information

Date

Time MICHELLE OBAMA

Inspired by Michelle Obama Quotes

A STORY IS WHAT WE HAVE AND WILL ALWAYS HAVE, IT IS SOMETHING FOR US TO OWN;
ARE WE GOOD ENOUGH? YES, OF COURSE WE ARE AND WE SHOULD KNOW
WE ARE NEVER ALONE.

IF THERE'S ONE THING WE SHOULD LEARN IN LIFE IT'S THE POWER OF USING THE VOICE;
EVEN IF WE DON'T WIN, IT'S THE PROGRESS WE MAKE THAT MATTERS,
AS WE FIGHT FOR THE FREEDOM OF CHOICE.
THERE IS SO MUCH WE DON'T KNOW ABOUT LIFE OR WHAT THE FUTURE WILL BRING,
BUT WE CAN TRULY BEGIN TO KNOW OURSELVES;
WE CAN BE MORE IN CHARGE OF OUR HAPPINESS AND PLANT THE SEEDS OF CHANGE,
AS WE LOOK AFTER EACH OTHER AND OUR OWN HEALTH.

THERE IS GRACE IN BEING WILLING TO KNOW AND HEAR OTHERS,
THERE IS POWER IN ALLOWING OURSELVES TO BE KNOWN AND HEARD;
BECOMING ISN'T ABOUT ARRIVING, IT'S A FORWARD MOTION TO KEEP EVOLVING
IT'S A JOURNEY TO BE BETTER AND HAVE CONVICTION BEHIND EACH WORD.
LIFE WILL TEACH US THAT PROGRESS AND CHANGE HAPPENS SLOWLY,
WE HAVE TO BE PATIENT AS WE BREATHE IN AND OUT;
THROUGHOUT LIFE WE MEET PEOPLE WHO HAVE ACHIEVED AND
DARED TO DREAM AND BELIEVE,
EACH ONE OF THEM WAS QUESTIONED AND SURROUNDED BY DOUBT.
CARING TOO MUCH ABOUT WHAT OTHERS THINK CAN BE A PROBLEM,
ON THE PATH THERE ARE OTHER WAYS AND PLACES TO BE;
IT'S ONE THING TO GET OURSELVES UNSTUCK FROM A PLACE THAT
HOLDS US DOWN,
IT'S MUCH HARDER FOR US TO SET A STUCK PLACE FREE.

@allontheboard

Service information

Date **MUHAMMAD**

Time **ALI**

(INSPIRED BY HIS QUOTES)

@allontheboard

DON'T COUNT THE DAYS; MAKE THE DAYS COUNT,
FLOAT LIKE A BUTTERFLY, STING LIKE A BEE;
IF OUR MINDS CAN CONCEIVE AND OUR HEARTS CAN BELIEVE,
THEN WE CAN ACHIEVE ANYTHING,
          IN A WORLD OF YOUR OWN SET YOURSELF FREE.

SOMEONE WHO HAS NO IMAGINATION HAS NO WINGS,
IT ISN'T THE MOUNTAIN THAT WEARS US OUT,
                    IT'S THE PEBBLE IN THE SHOE;
IF YOU FEEL DEFEATED REACH DOWN TO THE BOTTOM OF YOUR SOUL AND
                    YOU WILL FIND SOME EXTRA POWER,
DON'T WASTE YEARS OF YOUR LIFE NOT LEARNING AND HAVING THE SAME VIEW.

IMPOSSIBLE IS NOT A FACT, IT'S JUST AN OPINION,
IF WE ARE COURAGEOUS WE CAN ACCOMPLISH ANYTHING
                              WITH OUR LIVES ON EARTH;
LIVE EVERY DAY AS IF IT WAS YOUR LAST, BECAUSE SOMEDAY
                         YOU WILL BE RIGHT,
DON'T QUIT, EVEN THOUGH YOU MAY SUFFER,
YOU ARE A CHAMPION, PLEASE KNOW WHAT YOU'RE WORTH.

@allontheboard

Service information

Date   NELSON

Time   <u>MANDELA</u>

A WINNER IS A DREAMER WHO NEVER GIVES UP,
IT ALWAYS SEEMS IMPOSSIBLE UNTIL IT'S DONE;
LET YOUR OWN LIGHT SHINE, KEEP YOUR FEET MOVING FORWARD,
AND KEEP YOUR HEAD POINTED TOWARDS THE SUN.

WHEN PEOPLE ARE DETERMINED THEY CAN OVERCOME ANYTHING,
THERE IS NO EASY WALK TO FREEDOM ANYWHERE;
LET YOUR GREATNESS BLOSSOM, BE THE CAPTAIN OF YOUR SOUL,
GIVE A CHILD LOVE, LAUGHTER AND PEACE BY SHOWING YOU CARE.

WE CAN CHANGE THE WORLD AND MAKE IT A BETTER PLACE,
                        IT'S IN OUR HANDS TO MAKE A DIFFERENCE,
WE NEVER LOSE, WE EITHER WIN OR LEARN;
THERE IS NO GREATER GIFT THAN GIVING YOUR TIME AND ENERGY
                                    HELPING OTHERS,
WITHOUT EXPECTING ANYTHING IN RETURN.

— INSPIRED BY QUOTES FROM
<u>NELSON MANDELA</u>

@allontheboard

Service information

Date **PRINCE** ☥

Time 1958-2016

by @allontheboard

WHEN DOVES CRY SOFT AND WET TEARS INTO THE HOLY RIVER,
IT'S A SIGN O' THE TIMES THAT MONEY DON'T MATTER 2 NIGHT;
THE CINNAMON GIRL WORE PINK CASHMERE AND A RASPBERRY BERET,
EVERY SWEET KISS FROM HER LIPS TASTED JUST RIGHT.
AFTER THE PURPLE RAIN HAS FALLEN FROM THE GREY CLOUDS AND
                    THE THUNDER IS OVER,

MYSTERIOUSLY I'M DELIRIOUS AND U MAKE MY SUN SHINE;
IN THE MORNING PAPERS A ROCK AND ROLL LOVE AFFAIR
                    SEEMED LIKE THE GREATEST ROMANCE EVER SOLD,
IT WAS SCANDALOUS HOW THE TRUTH WAS LEFT OUT OF EVERY LINE.
THIEVES IN THE TEMPLE OF GOLD MAY TRY TO STEAL DIAMONDS AND PEARLS,
JUST LIKE THE MOST BEAUTIFUL GIRL IN THE WORLD MAY STEAL SOMEONE'S HEART,
LET'S GO CRAZY IN LAS VEGAS AND LET'S PRETEND WE'RE MARRIED,
I TOLD YOU I WOULD DIE 4 U RIGHT FROM THE START.
ALL ACROSS AMERICA SHORE TO SHORE, FROM NYC TO BALTIMORE,
FIND THE SPACE IN POP LIFE TO LETITGO AND FREE URSELF;
IF I WAS YOUR GIRLFRIEND I KNOW I COULD NEVER TAKE THE PLACE OF YOUR MAN.

NOTHING COMPARES 2 U, U GOT THE LOOK THAT WOULD FLY FROM A SHELF
A LITTLE RED CORVETTE MIGHT BREAKDOWN FROM TOO MANY
                    DAYSOF WILD BEHAVIOUR UPTOWN;
1999 SEEMED LIKE THE FUTURE IN A CRYSTAL BALL TO THE PARTYMAN;
I WISH YOU HEAVEN WHERE YOU ARE, MAY THE ARMS OF ORION EMBRACE YOU LIKE A STAR,
OUR TRIP AROUND THE WORLD IN A DAY DIDN'T QUITE GO TO PLAN.
THE NEW POWER GENERATION CREATED THE SPARK THAT MOVED MOUNTAINS IN PAISLEY PARK,
LOVE LETTERS CAUSED CONTROVERSY WHEN THEY GOT MIXED UP ON ALPHABET ST.;
"; NAME IS PRINCE AND I WANNA BE YOUR LOVER" SAID THE GLAM SLAM CHARMER
                    TO THE PRINCESS,
"BETCHA BY GOLLY WOW!, YOU'RE A PEACH AND YOU MAKE ME COMPLETE"
FOR YOU THE CREAM WILL RISE TO THE TOP, GETT OFF ON THE BATDANCE AND DON'T
                    STOP,
IN 7 LOVESEXY SECONDS SHOW THE WORLD WHAT YOU'RE WORTH;
AN XPECTATION OF EMANCIPATION CAUSED CHAOS AND DISORDER DURING THE PARADE,
THE LOVE SYMBOL PAINTED ON GRAFFITI BRIDGE SPOKE FOR PLANET EARTH.

Service information

Date

Time *Princess Diana* ♥

(INSPIRED BY QUOTES FROM 'THE QUEEN OF OUR HEARTS')

CARRY OUT A RANDOM ACT OF KINDNESS,
ONE DAY SOMEONE MIGHT DO THE SAME FOR YOU;

IF YOU FIND SOMEONE TO LOVE IN LIFE, HANG ON TO THEM,

ONLY DO WHAT YOUR HEART TELLS YOU TO.

EVERY PERSON IN THIS WORLD NEEDS TO FEEL VALUED AND LOVED,

EVERY ONE OF US CAN GIVE SOMETHING BACK;

KINDNESS, LOVE AND AFFECTION CAN HELP TO EASE ANY JOURNEY,

SHOW HOW MUCH WE CARE AND NOT FOCUS ON WHAT WE LACK.

UNDERSTAND OTHER PEOPLE'S STRESS, EMOTIONS AND INSECURITIES,

WHEN WE ARE HAPPY WE CAN LEARN HOW TO FORGIVE;

HUGS CAN DO SO MUCH GOOD, ESPECIALLY FOR CHILDREN,
MAY YOUR SPIRIT BE FREE IN HOW YOU CHOOSE TO LIVE.

@allontheboard

Service information

Date

Time *Roald Dahl*

1916 - 1990

by @allontheboard

IT DOESN'T MATTER IF YOU'RE DANNY, THE CHAMPION OF THE WORLD,
A DOCTOR, A CHILD OR A BUILDER;
EVERYONE IS SMITTEN WITH THE STORIES THAT WERE WRITTEN,
FROM THE MAGIC FINGER, GOING SOLO TO MATILDA.

WE LOVE THEM ALL TO BITS, THE FANTASTIC MR. FOX
AND THE TWITS,
REVOLTING RHYMES AND DIRTY BEASTS HAVE US IN STITCHES;
JAMES AND THE GIANT PEACH SHOWED US THE HEIGHTS WE COULD REACH
WITH A LITTLE FEAR THROWN IN BY THE WITCHES.

GEORGE'S MARVELLOUS MEDICINE COULDN'T TAKE THE PAIN AWAY,
BUT, BOY OH BOY, IT CERTAINLY RAISED A SMILE;
THE GIRAFFE AND THE PELLY AND ME WERE DOUBLED UP WITH GLEE,
READING THE BFG WITH THE ENORMOUS CROCODILE.

CHARLIE AND THE CHOCOLATE FACTORY WAS A PERFECT DREAM,
CHARLIE AND THE GREAT GLASS ELEVATOR TRAVELLED TO THE STARS;
WITH PURE IMAGINATION WE TELL TALES OF THE UNEXPECTED,
CHITTY CHITTY BANG BANG IS IN EVERYBODY'S LIST
OF TOP TEN CARS.

@allontheboard

Service information

Date

Time

SIR CHARLIE CHAPLIN   1889 - 1977

A DAY WITHOUT LAUGHTER
IS A DAY WASTED,
YOU'LL NEVER FIND A RAINBOW
IF YOU'RE LOOKING DOWN;
FAILURE IS UNIMPORTANT,
IT TAKES COURAGE TO MAKE
A FOOL OF YOURSELF,
WALKING AWAY FROM THE CIRCUS.
IN THE RAIN CAN HIDE
THE TEARS OF A CLOWN.
WE THINK TOO MUCH AND FEEL TOO LITTLE,
IN THESE MODERN TIMES,
IMAGINATION MEANS NOTHING WITHOUT DOING;
IT'S SAD TO GET USED TO LUXURY,
LAUGHTER IS THE TONIC AND IT'S THE KEY,
TO OPEN UP EVERY LOCKED DOOR IN EAST STREET
TO HOLLYWOOD OR ON THE ROAD TO RUIN.
FROM A KID TO A TRAMP AND THE GREAT DICTATOR,
AN ACTOR, A DIRECTOR AND AN OSCAR WINNER,
THE CITY LIGHTS COULD NEVER STEAL THE LIMELIGHT
FROM WHAT YOU COULD DO;
HAPPY HEAVENLY BIRTHDAY TO YOU CHARLIE CHAPLIN,
THANKS FOR THE SMILE
YOU GAVE TO THE WORLD
AND FOR BEING YOU.

@allontheboard

Service information

Date
Time

STEPHEN HAWKING
(1942 - 2018)

YOU SAID IF YOU COULD BE A HERO YOU WOULD BE SUPERMAN,
TO PLANET EARTH YOU WERE A HERO AND SUPER;
DEFYING LIMITATIONS, AN INSPIRATION ACROSS EACH NATION,
FROM STAR TREK GENERATIONS AND THE SIMPSONS TO SHELDON COOPER.
FROM THE BIG BANG THEORY TO THE THEORY OF EVERYTHING,
YOU SAID THE UNIVERSE IS EXPANDING;
FROM A BRIEF HISTORY OF TIME YOU SUMMED UP THE UNIVERSE IN A NUTSHELL,
EVEN WHEN OTHER MINDS HAD TROUBLE UNDERSTANDING.
THE LIMITATIONS OF DISABILITY DIDN'T STOP YOU FLOATING IN ZERO GRAVITY,
'THERE GOES MY HERO' FOO FIGHTERS WILL SING;
MAY YOU FIND TRUE FREEDOM IN PARADISE, TO DISCOVER THE MEANING OF LIFE,
FROM WALKING ON MARS TO EXPLORING SATURN'S RING.
'WE ARE ALL DIFFERENT, BUT WE SHARE THE SAME HUMAN SPIRIT,
PERHAPS IT'S HUMAN NATURE THAT WE ADAPT AND SURVIVE;'
LET'S ALL BE CHILDREN OF NATURE AND KEEP ASKING THE QUESTIONS,
STARTING WITH 'HOW' AND 'WHY' WE ARE ALIVE.
FOR ETERNITY YOU WILL BE REMEMBERED AS A GENIUS AND A LEGEND,
MAY YOUR SEARCH FOR A NEW EARTH BE OVER, WHEREVER YOU ARE;
ALS DIDN'T PREVENT YOU FROM ROCKING SCIENCE AND THE MIND'S POTENTIAL,
AND IN THE SKY AT NIGHT YOU WILL BE THE GALAXY'S BRIGHTEST STAR.

REST IN PEACE STEPHEN HAWKING.

@allontheboard

Service information

Date William
Time Shakespeare

MEASURE FOR MEASURE EVERY HENRY FROM 4 TO 8 WAS GREAT,
THE DISCO WAS A MIDSUMMER NIGHT'S DREAM;
ALL OF THE MERRY WIVES OF WINDSOR WERE DANCING AS YOU LIKE IT,
THEN CAME A COMEDY OF ERRORS WHEN ONE SLIPPED ON
                              DROPPED ICE CREAM.
LOVE'S LABOUR'S LOST BUT IT KNOWS WHERE YOU ARE,
HAMLET LOVED THE OCCASIONAL CELEBRATORY CIGAR,
THE MERCHANT OF VENICE ENJOYED PLAYING TENNIS WITH
                              CORIOLANUS AND CYMBELINE;
ROMEO AND JULIET KEPT THEIR SOCIAL DISTANCE ON BALCONIES,
BY THE TWELFTH NIGHT ANTONY AND CLEOPATRA
                              WERE EXPERTS AT QUARANTINE.
JULIUS CAESAR WAS A GEEZER AND COULDN'T WAIT TO HAVE A BEER
WITH THE TWO GENTLEMEN OF VERONA, KING JOHN AND KING LEAR,
FOR HE'S A JOLLY GOOD OTHELLO SO SAY TITUS ANDRONICUS;
RICHARD THE SECOND HAD A WORD WITH RICHARD THE THIRD
                              ABOUT THE TAMING OF THE SHREW,
IT'S MUCH ADO ABOUT NOTHING WHEN THERE'S NOTHING MUCH TO DO,
WHEN MACBETH LOST HIS BREATH HE GAVE IN TO THE TEMPEST
                              IN THE FORM OF A BUS.
PERICLES COULD BE A NERVOUS WRECK WHEN HE PACED THE DECK,
HIS FRIEND TIMON OF ATHENS WOULD SORT HIM OUT WHEN THEY SET SAIL;
ALL'S WELL THAT ENDS WELL BEING SAVED BY THE BELL,
TROILUS AND CRESSIDA KEPT EACH OTHER WARM DURING THE WINTER'S TALE.

@allontheboard

Service information

Date <u>JOHN LENNON</u>
1940 - 1980

Time

WELL WELL WELL , LOOK AT ME, I LOVE HOW MOTHER NATURE
SHOWS ME BEAUTY WHEN I'M LOST AT SEA,
POWER TO THE PEOPLE WHO REMEMBER TO HOLD ON TO HOPE IN EVERY TOUGH SITUATION;
I FOUND OUT UNFINISHED MUSIC DREAMS OF A STAGE,
FLICKING THROUGH THE WEDDING ALBUM GAVE PLEASURE PAGE AFTER PAGE,
A WORKING CLASS HERO MAY SPEND SOME TIME IN NEW YORK CITY FOR ISOLATION.
IT'S SO HARD WHEN A JEALOUS GUY FEELS CRIPPLED INSIDE
I DON'T WANNA BE A SOLDIER OR STRUGGLE WITH PRIDE,
OH MY LOVE GIMME SOME TRUTH AND LET ME WORK ON A PROMISE TO KEEP;
OH YOKO! I KNOW I'VE BEEN LOW FOR SO LONG,
IMAGINE HOW? A MELODY IN A MINOR KEY WOULD FEEL WITH THE WRONG SONG,
EVEN THE VOICE IN MY HEAD TENDERLY ASKS ME, "HOW DO YOU SLEEP?"
A MAP POINTS OUT TO ME YOU ARE HERE IN MEAT CITY,
WHEN MY INTUITION PLAYS MIND GAMES WITH ME,
I KNOW (I KNOW) I SHOULD TAKE ONE DAY (AT A TIME) TO LIVE;
AISUMASEN (I'M SORRY) FOR MY MUSCLES BEING AS TIGHT A$ A SCREW,
REAL LOVE IS A DRAMA WITH INSTANT KARMA (WE ALL SHINE ON) FROM OUT THE BLUE,
WE ARE ONLY PEOPLE AND SHOULD TAKE AS MUCH AS WE GIVE.
BLESS YOU IF YOU THINK NOBODY LOVES YOU (WHEN YOU'RE DOWN AND OUT),
ALONG THE OLD DIRT ROAD DO WHATEVER GETS YOU THRU THE NIGHT
WHEN THE SUN IS GOING DOWN ON LOVE;
DON'T BE SCARED IF THE SURPRISE SURPRISE (SWEET BIRD OF PARADOX)
MAY PINCH YOUR BEEF JERKY, SAY "YA YA" AND QUESTION WHAT YOU GOT,
IN A #9 DREAM STEEL AND GLASS WALLS AND BRIDGES TOWERED ABOVE.
DEAR YOKO IS A WOMAN WITH A BEAUTIFUL BOY (DARLING BOY),
NOBODY TOLD ME WATCHING THE WHEELS IN CLEANUP TIME WOULD BRING ME JOY,
(FORGIVE ME) MY LITTLE FLOWER PRINCESS I DON'T WANNA FACE IT IF I'M LOSING YOU;
I'M STEPPING OUT AND DRINKING MILK AND HONEY IN A DOUBLE FANTASY,
HAPPY XMAS (WAR IS OVER), GIVE PEACE A CHANCE WITH COLD TURKEY,
STAND BY ME WITH BORROWED TIME, BECAUSE (JUST LIKE) STARTING OVER
@allontheboard   IS ALL WE SEEM TO DO.

What does it mean to be a hero? All it takes is just one moment of kindness. Kindness can make somebody feel better, it can turn a life around or save someone's life. We all have it within ourselves to be kind, therefore we can all be heroes. Some people choose to be heroes by helping out those who are less fortunate than themselves, raising money for charities, raising awareness of illnesses and conditions, and saving lives. Others care for people, protect lives and try to make the world a better place.

There have been heroes throughout history who have made the ultimate sacrifice, those who have either risked or lost their lives by fighting for their countries and for the freedom of others. Their selfless acts of heroism should be remembered and honoured. But you don't have to be extraordinary to be a hero. Being able to fly, shoot lasers from eyes and jump over tall buildings with a single leap would all be great abilities to have, but they aren't necessary for becoming a hero (although they do look great on a cinema screen and in comic books).

Small acts of selflessness can be heroic – from helping someone to cross the road, to providing listening ears and an open heart for anyone who needs someone to talk to. You may not be rewarded or widely recognised for these small deeds, and it's easy to think you haven't changed the world, but you will have changed someone's world by doing something kind. If more of us do this, then the world could change for the better.

We consider members of our family to be heroes, for being who they are and doing what they do. They will know who we are talking about as they read this (and if they are not reading this, even with a family discount on the book, they won't be our heroes for much longer).

Our 'real' jobs working for Transport for London often put us in circumstances where we find ourselves reuniting lost travellers with family and friends, assisting mobility-impaired and visually-impaired people to get around, being there for vulnerable people and showing compassion and care to those who may need it.

We have each talked people out of committing suicide when we have been at work, despite not being counsellors. Yes, we are doing our jobs and getting paid but we often need to go beyond the call of duty, like many colleagues we know, and it's always worth it.

There are many heroes in the world going beyond the call of duty too. Here are some of those we consider to be real-life heroes.

A few years ago I was working on a very busy evening shift at peak time at King's Cross St Pancras. Surrounded by hundreds of people, I spotted a lady who I can only describe as 'out of place'. By that, I mean that something was clearly not right, and yet so easily ignored by everyone else but me. I still cannot place what it was, all I knew was I needed to speak with her and to do that would be a good thing. So I did. A simple 'Hello, are you okay?' That was all. Her reply, after a very long pause, was 'No, I'm not'.

Almost an hour later I was still with her in the station, away from the crowd and with other professionals for support. I had convinced her not to do something to herself that would have likely been permanent. Was that heroic? I don't know. We are paid to look out for the safety of all who use the London Underground, it's our job. But it doesn't matter – what matters is that an entire life that may have been lost is still here.

I've met real-life heroes: firefighters, nurses, paramedics and others. Heroes surround us, and yet sometimes there seems to be so few. Maybe because we don't see them? Perhaps it's because we forget what they are?

We consistently see comic book heroes in outlandish adventures that excite and blow our minds. There are some fantastical people who are heroes, but many are not. Most don't wear capes, and they're not superhuman or impossibly good looking. They could be absolutely anyone at any moment, and can appear when you least expect it.

Even you could be one and not even know it yet. A tiny feat from you may already be etched in the mind of someone who looks at you in a way that is filled with awe and happiness, a feat that to them is heroic. That makes you very important.

To children, those closest to them can be their heroes for the smallest thing that seems nothing more than a simple gesture: their mum or dad checking for gremlins under the bed before they sleep is courage unlike anything they see anywhere else. That's heroic too.

By definition, a real-life hero is someone who puts others first, sacrificing themselves for the good of others with no thought of reward. It does not mean rewards cannot come to them. It doesn't mean they cannot accept them. But their actions are not motivated by them.

This chapter is dedicated to all those real-life heroes out there, not just those who we have been able to include but also those we haven't.

Service information

Date **100 YEARS OF**
Time **WOMEN'S SUFFRAGE**

WOMEN ARE NOT THE MINORITY, THEY DESERVE EQUALITY,
THEY ARE HALF THE POPULATION OF THIS EARTH;
WHY SHOULD THEY HAVE TO JUSTIFY OR FIGHT FOR
EQUAL PAY AND RIGHTS,
THERE'S NO NEED FOR THEM TO PROVE WHAT THEY ARE WORTH.

AS WE CELEBRATE 100 YEARS THAT BRAVE WOMEN,
WENT THROUGH BLOOD, SWEAT AND TEARS,
TO CHANGE THE COURSE OF HISTORY AND THE RIGHT TO VOTE;
THERE'S STILL SO MUCH TO DO, IT'S UP TO YOU AND ME TOO,
TO MAKE A CHANGE WITH A MESSAGE TO PROMOTE.

@allontheboard

Service information

Date
Time **CARERS**

by
@allontheboard

IT IS ONLY NATURAL TO FEEL STRESSED
    IF EVERY DAY YOU HELP SOMEONE GET OUT OF BED
                AND GET THEM DRESSED,
YOU MAY CLEAN THEM, FEED THEM AND
                ASSIST WITH EACH EVERYDAY TASK;
IT CAN BE LONELY, ISOLATING AND FRUSTRATING,
    GIVING ALL YOUR TIME AND ENERGY TO EASE
                            SOMEONE'S
SITUATION,
BUT, YOU DO IT FOR LOVE AND NOTHING IS TOO MUCH TO ASK.

WE SEND OUR LOVE, HUGS AND THOUGHTS
        TO ALL OF THE CARERS IN THE WORLD,
WE RESPECT AND ADMIRE WHO YOU ARE AND
                        EVERYTHING YOU DO;
DON'T FORGET TO CARE FOR YOURSELF
        WHILE YOU ARE BUSY CARING FOR OTHERS
                    AND THEIR HEALTH,
PLEASE REACH OUT TO PEOPLE AND ORGANISATIONS
        WHEN YOU NEED SOME HELP AND SUPPORT TOO.

@allontheboard

Service information

Date HAPPY BIRTHDAY
Time KATIE PIPER

Love @allontheboard

HAPPY BIRTHDAY KATIE, WE HOPE YOU HAVE A LOVELY DAY,
MAY YOUR DREAMS AND WISHES ALL COME TRUE;
YOU ARE AMAZING AND AN INSPIRATION WITH
                              THE KATIE PIPER FOUNDATION,
IF YOU EVER COME THROUGH THE TUBE STATION
                    WE WOULD LOVE TO HAVE A SELFIE WITH YOU.
RAISING AWARENESS AND SECRET MILLIONS FOR CHARITY,
              A SUPERSTAR SPA AND SALON MANAGER ON HOTEL GB,
YOU PROVED YOU HAVE THE MOVES ON STRICTLY COME DANCING
                    AND ON TV YOU FAMOUSLY FOUGHT CRIME;
ON 20/20 WITH YOUR BEAUTIFUL FACE
                        YOU SHOWED THE SCIENCE OF SEEING,
SPREADING POSITIVITY AND ALTERNATIVE CHRISTMAS MESSAGES,
                YOU ARE A WONDERFUL HUMAN BEING.
AN ACTIVIST, A PRESENTER, A WRITER,
                    A WIFE, MOTHER AND A FIGHTER,
WITH A FONDNESS FOR FASHION AND BEAUTY AND
                    A NOMINEE FOR SO MANY AWARDS;
SHARING THE SECRET OF CONFIDENCE AND THE BELIEF TO SURVIVE,
THANKS FOR BEING YOURSELF AND FOR BEING ALIVE.
YOU DESERVE A BEAUTIFUL EVER AFTER
AND A POEM ON ONE OF OUR BOARDS.

@allontheboard

Service information

Date

Time HOSPICES

by @allontheboard

THEY HELP TO CREATE POSITIVE MEMORIES

AND MAKE MOMENTS MATTER,

BY PROVIDING MEDICAL, MENTAL AND EMOTIONAL SUPPORT

TO FAMILIES WHO ARE SHATTERED,

GIVING PEOPLE WITH LIFE THREATENING

AND LIFE LIMITING CONDITIONS

AROUND THE CLOCK CARE;

HOSPICES ARE NOT PLACES TO DIE,

THEY ARE LOVING PLACES TO FIND SOME PEACE AND RELIEF,

FROM HELPING LIVES LIMITED BY TIME

TO FAMILIES BROKEN-HEARTED BY GRIEF,

IN THE MOST DISTRESSING TIMES OF OUR LIVES

WE ALL NEED SOMEONE LIKE THEM

TO BE THERE.

UNDERGROUND Service information

Date **HAPPY BIRTHDAY**

Time **STACEY DOOLEY**

HAPPY BIRTHDAY STACEY DOOLEY MAY YOUR DREAMS AND WISHES COME TRUE;
YOU ARE SIMPLY WONDERFUL, YOU SPARKLE LIKE THE STRICTLY GLITTERBALL,
THANKS SO MUCH FOR DOING WHAT YOU DO.

YOU ARE A TRUE INSPIRATION, SHINING A LIGHT ON TERRIBLE SITUATIONS,
WITH YOUR REPORTS AND INVESTIGATIONS FROM THE FRONT LINE;
MAY YOU ENJOY YOUR BIRTHDAY BREAK
AND AFTER YOU'VE EATEN A SLICE OF CAKE,
SHOW OFF THE MOVES THAT MADE YOU THE BALLROOM CHAMPION
WITH A CHEEKY GLASS OF WINE.

YOU FIGHT FOR JUSTICE AND YOU SPEAK FOR THOSE WHO ARE OPPRESSED,
YOU WORK HARD AND NEVER SEEM TO REST,
THE WORLD IS BLESSED FOR HAVING SOMEONE LIKE YOU;
HAVE AN AMAZING DAY AND MAY LOADS OF GOOD THINGS
COME YOUR WAY,

WE REALLY HOPE YOU ENJOY BEING 32.

Love from @allontheboard
X

The joy of seeing our boards shared

It's not only the celebrity shares that have us stunned. From time to time we've seen our boards pop up on the TV and in newspapers. One board we wrote for Phillip Schofield's birthday was read out by Holly Willoughby on *This Morning*, and another we wrote about Stacey Solomon and Joe Swash found its way on to *Loose Women*. One we wrote about the England Lionesses at the FIFA Women's World Cup was also read out on BBC Sport before one of their matches, and Stacey Dooley even included one in a documentary about the NHS staff during the Coronavirus pandemic. Most of the time we don't know until one of our followers or friends spots it, so it's always a sudden and beautiful surprise.

Service information

Date AN
Time INESCAPABLE CHOICE
(INSPIRED BY THE WORDS OF SIR DAVID ATTENBOROUGH)

CLIMATE CHANGE IS OUR GREATEST THREAT IN THOUSANDS OF YEARS,
IT'S A MAN-MADE DISASTER ON A GLOBAL SCALE;
THE PEOPLE OF THE WORLD HAVE SPOKEN, THE MESSAGE IS CRYSTAL CLEAR,
DECISION MAKERS MUST ACT AND CANNOT FAIL.
WHY ARE WE HERE? HOW DO WE FIT IN? WHAT'S IT ALL ABOUT?
THE NATURAL WORLD IS THE GREATEST SOURCE THAT MAKES LIFE WORTH LIVING,
CLIMATE CHANGE IS HAPPENING RAPIDLY, HUMANS HAVE A PART TO PLAY,
THE WORLD IS A GIFT, BUT IT'S ONE THAT CAN'T ALWAYS KEEP GIVING.
IF ONLY THIS WORLD WAS TWICE AS BIG AND THERE WAS STILL SO MUCH TO EXPLORE,
EACH ANIMAL AND PLANT IS A SOLUTION TO THE PROBLEM OF STAYING ALIVE,
THE WORLD IS VALUABLE AND WONDERFUL, IT'S A PRECIOUS PLACE TO TREASURE,
IT'S UP TO US AND THE LEADERS OF THE WORLD TO HELP IT SURVIVE.
DEALING WITH GLOBAL WARMING DOESN'T MEAN WE SUDDENLY STOPPED BREATHING,
IT'S A CASE OF NOT WASTING AND BEARING THINGS IN MIND;
TO BE CURIOUS AND TO GAIN A BETTER UNDERSTANDING CAN LEAD TO GREAT FULFILMENT,
IT'S NOT NATURE'S INTENTION TO HARM US OR TO BE UNKIND.
AS HUMAN BEINGS WE CAN BE OBSESSED WITH OURSELVES AND OUR OWN HISTORY,
OPEN EYES WILL FIND THE CONSEQUENCES ARE NOT SURPRISING;
IF WE DON'T TAKE ACTION THE COLLAPSE OF CIVILIZATION MAY HAPPEN,
AS THE EXTINCTION OF THE NATURAL WORLD LOOMS ON THE HORIZON.

@allontheboard

UNDERGROUND

Service information

Date IT'S STILL NOT
Time TOO LATE TO ACT

INSPIRED BY THE WORDS OF GRETA THUNBERG

THE EYES OF ALL FUTURE GENERATIONS ARE UPON THEM,
HOW CAN WE FORGIVE THEM IF THEY CHOOSE TO FAIL,
                              KNOWING WHAT'S AT STAKE?
NOBODY IS EVER TOO SMALL OR TOO YOUNG
                    TO MAKE A DIFFERENCE,
RIGHT HERE, RIGHT NOW IS WHERE WE DRAW THE LINE,
                         FOR OUR OWN SAKE.
MAKE YOUR VOICES HEARD AND LET THE ECHOES HELP TO GIVE HOPE
                                    AND HEAL,
NEVER STOP FIGHTING FOR THE FUTURE AND PLANET EARTH;
TRANSFORM ANGER INTO ACTION, STAND UNITED AND NEVER GIVE UP,
FIND A MEANING IN A WORLD WHERE SOME PEOPLE
                    FORGET ITS TRUE MEANING AND WORTH.
WE NEED TO UNDERSTAND THE MESS THAT'S BEEN CREATED,
IT'S HARD TO STOP AND SMELL THE ROSES WITH SO MUCH POLLUTION;
WITH DETERMINATION, COURAGE AND A FAR-REACHING VISION,
                         IT'S STILL NOT TOO LATE TO ACT,
MAYBE CHANGE THE SYSTEM IF THE SYSTEM CAN'T FIND THE SOLUTION.
HOW CAN THE KIDS DREAM BIG AND THINK THE SKY IS THE LIMIT?
IF THEY ARE SOLD FALSE HOPE AND THE WORLD ISN'T FIT
                    FOR THEM TO LIVE IN IT,
IT'S SICKENING TO BELIEVE THE AIR THEY BREATHE IS STOLEN BY GREED;
CHILDREN ARE MAKING HEADLINES AS THEY STRIKE FOR CLIMATE,
IF WE LISTEN AND STAND TOGETHER WE CAN SUCCEED.
                    @allontheboard

Service information

Date LONDON'S
Time AIR AMBULANCE

SINCE 1989 LONDON'S AIR AMBULANCE HAS SERVED
THE 10 MILLION PEOPLE,
WHO LIVE, WORK AND TRAVEL WITHIN THE M25;
THESE DEDICATED TEAMS OF REAL LIFE SUPERHEROES
PROVIDE PRE-HOSPITAL CARE,
WORKING TIRELESSLY TO KEEP PEOPLE ALIVE.
ON A MISSION WITH A VISION, THEY ARE COMPASSIONATE,
COURAGEOUS AND PIONEERING,
THEY WANT TO SAVE TIME, THEY WANT TO SAVE LIVES AND PROVIDE BETTER CARE;
FROM 8 AM TO SUNSET IN A HELICOPTER OR RAPID RESPONSE CARS AT NIGHT,
WHEN TIME IS CRITICAL THEY WILL TAKE CALCULATED RISKS TO BE THERE.
FROM ROAD TRAFFIC COLLISIONS TO STABBINGS AND SHOOTINGS,
OPEN HEART SURGERY AND BLOOD TRANSFUSIONS,
THROUGH CHALLENGING WEATHER CONDITIONS LIKE THE RAIN, SNOW, FOG OR MIST;
WE NEED THEM TO KEEP SERVING LONDON WITH THEIR HEROIC LIFE SAVING,
BUT, THEY REALLY NEED OUR GENEROSITY TO EXIST.
WITHOUT OUR HELP TO FUND THEIR RUNNING COSTS
THEY CAN'T CONTINUE TO HELP PATIENTS,
THEY ARE A CHARITY WHICH RELY ON FUNDRAISING AND EACH DONATION;
ONE DAY IT MAY BE US OR A LOVED ONE
WHO NEEDS THEIR RAPID RESPONSE AND CARE,
TO PROVIDE EMERGENCY MEDICAL TREATMENT IN A LIFE OR DEATH SITUATION.

@allontheboard

Service information

Thank You to all of
the amazing midwives,
for who you are and
what you do,
You are professional,
passionate, courageous,
loving and you really
do care;
Working so hard to
deliver babies around
the clock and
looking after mothers,
It doesn't matter what's
going on in the world,
You are always there.

@allontheboard

Service information

NURSES ARE TRULY HEROES
DOING A JOB THAT MOST COULDN'T DO,
HEALING IS THEIR MISSION AND
                 COMPASSION IS THEIR POWER;
THROUGH THE DARK TIMES THEY SMILE
          AND THEIR LIGHT SHINES THROUGH,
COURAGEOUS AND READY FOR ACTION
WITH TENDER LOVING CARE
DURING ANY DARKEST HOUR.
WITHOUT FUSS THEY TAKE GOOD CARE OF US,
THEY COMFORT WITH PROFESSIONALISM,
KIND WORDS AND LISTENING EARS;
SHOWING THE BEST OF HUMANITY
AND HELPING TO EASE ANXIETY,
WARMING EVERY HEART WITH KINDNESS
AND HIDING THEIR OWN WORRIES AND FEARS.
DISPLAYING PATIENCE WITH PATIENTS
IN MOMENTS OF FRUSTRATION,
THEY FULLY DESERVE OUR APPRECIATION,
ALWAYS THERE IN SICKNESS AND HEALTH,
                 FOR BETTER OR WORSE;
WORKING SO HARD DAY AND NIGHT
TO MAKE THINGS ALRIGHT, PROVING
LOVE AND CARING IS THE ESSENCE OF LIFE,
IT TAKES A SPECIAL PERSON
TO BE A NURSE.

Service information

SUPERHEROES DON'T NEED TO WEAR CAPES,
THEY JUST NEED TO DISPLAY KINDNESS
AND THE RIGHT KIND OF HUMAN BEHAVIOUR;
WE CAN ALL BE HEROES LIKE
PATRICK HUTCHINSON
AND IN ONE MOMENT BECOME
SOMEBODY'S SAVIOUR.

@allontheboard

Service information

Date

Time **POPPY**

REMEMBER THOSE WHO GAVE THEIR LIVES IN BATTLE,
BY WEARING THE FLOWER THAT GREW ON THE FIELDS,
AFTER WORLD WAR ONE;
THESE BRAVE SOLDIERS FOUGHT FOR OUR FREEDOM
AND ANSWERED THE CALL OF DUTY,
AND TODAY WE PLAY CALL OF DUTY FOR FUN.
FOREVER YOUNG, FOREVER LOVED, FOREVER IN OUR HEARTS,
LET'S SHOW OUR GRATITUDE AND RESPECT
WITH A MOMENT OF SILENCE;
WEAR A POPPY WITH PRIDE AND TOGETHER ABIDE
TO STOP ALL THE WARS AND THE VIOLENCE.

@allontheboard

Service information

SUPER PARENTS

WE LOVE OUR SUPERHEROES IN COMIC BOOKS,
AND ON THE CINEMA SCREEN;
BUT, I BET THEY COULDN'T DEAL WITH US,
WHEN WE'RE GOING THROUGH OUR DIFFICULT TEENS.
WOULD IRON MAN IRON YOUR CLOTHES,
AND MAKE YOU A PACKED LUNCH FOR SCHOOL?
WOULD SUPERMAN TEACH YOU ABOUT THE BIRDS AND THE BEES?
AND HOW BEING RUDE ISN'T COOL.

WOULD CAPTAIN AMERICA TAKE YOU ON HOLIDAYS,
AND TREAT YOU TO ICE CREAM OR A TOY?
WOULD WONDER WOMAN CUDDLE YOU IN HER ARMS,
IF YOU'VE HAD YOUR HEARTBROKEN BY A GIRL OR A BOY?

WOULD THE FLASH LEND YOU CASH TO PAY BILLS,
OR WHENEVER PUSH COMES TO SHOVE?
WOULD BATMAN ALWAYS WATCH OVER YOU,
AND PROTECT YOU WITH UNCONDITIONAL LOVE?
WOULD THOR KISS YOUR HEAD, MAKE YOUR DINNER AND YOUR BED,
AND GET YOU BETTER WHEN YOU'RE FEELING BAD?
WOULD THE INCREDIBLE HULK, THROW A TANTRUM AND SULK?
BECAUSE HE DOESN'T COMPARE TO YOUR DAD.

WOULD BLACK PANTHER BE PROUD OF YOUR ACHIEVEMENTS,
AND SHOW IT WITH A PUMP OF A FIST?
IN EARTH AND IN HEAVEN, WE ARE LUCKY TO HAVE THEM,
SUPER PARENTS DO TRULY EXIST.

@allontheboard

Service information

Date **FOR**

Time **RACHAEL BLAND**

WE CAN ALL MAKE A DIFFERENCE WITH OUR TIME ON EARTH,
AND MAKE THE WORLD A BETTER PLACE;
RACHAEL BLAND, YOU HAVE DONE SO MUCH FOR SO MANY PEOPLE,
WITH STYLE, HUMOUR AND GRACE.

EVEN IN DEATH THERE IS LAUGHTER TO BE FOUND,
YOU HAVE BATTLED CANCER SO BRAVELY AND WITH DIGNITY;
A BRILLIANT MUM, WIFE AND BROADCASTER HELPING OTHERS TO COPE,
SHOWING AMAZING COURAGE IN THE FACE OF ADVERSITY.

NOTHING IN LIFE IS CERTAIN, ONLY WE ALL FACE THE FINAL CURTAIN,
WE ARE INSPIRED BY YOU AND AS YOUR NEXT ADVENTURE BEGINS;
PLEASE KNOW YOU HAVE CHANGED THE NATION'S CONVERSATION
                              WITH YOUR STORY AND INSPIRATION
IN EVERY CANCER BATTLE IT'S ALWAYS LOVE THAT WINS.

EVERYBODY IN THE WORLD NEEDS TO HEAR YOUR VOICE AND STORY,
THE PODCAST DESERVES TO BE AT NUMBER ONE IN THE CHARTS;
YOUR LEGACY WILL LIVE ON AND INSPIRE SO MANY OTHERS,
AND YOU WILL LIVE ON IN MEMORIES AND SO MANY HEARTS.

@allontheboard

Rachael Bland

In 2018, we discovered the voices of three women with cancer and an inseparable bond and strength that led them to create the award-winning podcast, 'You, Me and the Big C'. Rachael Bland – a phenomenal woman, parent, journalist and blogger – was one of the three, and she sadly died that year of cancer.

After reading her tweet stating that she had just days left, we felt compelled to write her a poem. We wanted her to know her message of hope and her honesty and work had saved countless lives, and helped even more readers and listeners to know how to live with cancer.

It was a personal poem, as well as a way of projecting her to those on the Tube living with this invisible condition. We were later informed that she had seen the poem and we hope she liked it.

BBC Radio invited us to talk about the poem and I (EI) was proud to do that but had to do so on my own (NI was suffering with a relapse of his ulcerative colitis at the time). I was interviewed and then I read the poem on the show, explaining its purpose and the hopes behind it.

It is one of the most important poems we have ever written, its impact for us has been clear; we truly hope it was for Rachael too.

Service information

Date

Time TEACHERS

I'M AN INFORMATION BOARD AND ATTENDED BOARDING SCHOOL,
THEY WERE THE BEST DAYS OF MY LIFE,
                    BUT, AT THE TIME THEY WEREN'T SO COOL;
WHEN I PAID NO ATTENTION, I GOT A DETENTION
                    IT REALLY WAS MY OWN TIME I WOULD WASTE,
OH DEAR, I'VE JUST HAD A FLASHBACK TO SOME SCHOOL DINNERS,
                    THEY COULD BE AN ACQUIRED TASTE.

HOW MANY TIMES HAS A TEACHER HEARD
                    'MY HOMEWORK WAS EATEN BY THE DOG'?
DON'T HAVE TOO MANY LATE SCHOOL NIGHTS,
                    WHEN YOU SHOULD BE SLEEPING LIKE A LOG.
WHEN THE TEACHERS ASK QUESTIONS DON'T TREMBLE OR WORRY
                    OR PRETEND TO BE INVISIBLE IN CLASS;
IF YOU DON'T KNOW THE ANSWER, JUST SIMPLY SAY
                    'I'M SORRY, I DON'T KNOW, I WILL JUST HAVE TO PASS.'

THEY ARE TRYING TO GUIDE US WITH MATHS, ENGLISH AND SCIENCE,
HISTORY, GEOGRAPHY, GERMAN AND FRENCH;
YOU CAN STILL HAVE FUN, BUT, SHOW SOME RESPECT,
BY NOT THROWING TANTRUMS AND CAUSING A STENCH
TEACHERS ARE MINDERS, THEY ARE THERE TO GUIDE US.
IF WE DO WELL THEY ARE EVER SO PLEASED,
THERE WILL COME A TIME WHEN YOU LOOK BACK WITH NOSTALGIA
AND DISCUSS THEM WITH FOND MEMORIES.

@allontheboard

Service information

THANK YOU NHS,
WE ARE GRATEFUL AND
APPRECIATE EVERYTHING YOU DO;
        THE HARD WORKING STAFF
        AND THE FREE HEALTHCARE,
WHERE WOULD WE BE WITHOUT YOU?

FOR 71 YEARS
YOU HAVE BEEN LOOKING AFTER US
AND
HELPING TO KEEP US ALIVE,
YOU ARE THE HEARTBEAT
AND
THE BLOOD OF THIS NATION,
WE NEED TO PROTECT YOU
        AND HELP YOU SURVIVE.

@allontheboard

9

Occasions & Celebrations

Any opportunity we get to celebrate with one another in unity and to try to create magical memories and fond moments to remember, we should always make the most of, whether it's sporting events, anniversaries, birthdays or happy occasions.

It feels good to be happy.

It feels even better when you're feeling happy and many others are feeling the same way too.

Sharing is caring and all that jazz.

What an amazing feeling it is to feel a part of something and possibly creating history, making history or being involved in something that will be forever remembered in history.

Or even just an excuse to have a bit of a dance and a laugh with others. It's all groovy.

We all live our own lives and there are times when it can feel like a lonely existence, so we really should embrace every moment that brings us together.

To be on the same side. United.

Through good times, we want to celebrate together. Through bad times, we want to stand together and support one another. That's the way that it should be.

Working for TfL at underground stations during the London Olympics in 2012 was an absolutely amazing time, definitely one of my highlights of working for TfL.

London was absolutely buzzing. People coming from all over the world to cheer on their home countries competing against one another. It was a joy to be a part of and, if I had my way, London would host the Olympics every six months, even though it happens every four years. It was magical. But, it's only fair to share the magic around the world.

When we put one of our poem boards at a station next to a venue where an artist is performing, it seems to be the cherry on the top of a delicious cake for excited fans going to that event. It's a good feeling for us to be able add to their excitement and happiness as we watch people take photos with the boards.

Celebrate good times, come on.

The first board we ever wrote was for a concert. Since then we have written over 300 poems for events of all kinds.

Each time we have tried to improve them and push ourselves to write in more elaborate and connected ways.

Sometimes we get a second go. The likes of Ed Sheeran, Little Mix, The Script, Olly Murs and many others have returned more than once. We love events of all kinds, from music to sports and comedy. We love to write about all of them equally and we will keep on doing so for as long as we can.

Occasions and celebrations can bring people together, bridge divides and provide a chance to experience other cultures. They offer a moment to focus on something good and comforting and if it's a regular occurence even more so. From the World Cup to Mother's Day, there are so many things worth celebrating for the joy they bring.

My favourite board from this chapter is the one we wrote for exam results. It's a part of my life I remember vividly and I still consider it one of the most stressful times. Its impact on mental health cannot be ignored. Recognising this moment for those taking exams and their parents is so important. Geniuses have failed at school and become successes. Look at Picasso's famous troubles with art at school? Even mega stars like Tom Cruise and Cameron Diaz had problems in school. Exam results are only one avenue to success, and I know from my own results that I struggled in the things I was always considered talented in and am vastly more successful in than they showed.

Then there are those occasions where people celebrate as they go through our stations, like New Year's Eve or the London Olympics. Yes, they add pressure to our job but they are also filled with beautiful moments of joy amongst strangers from all walks of life, recognising that they're sharing a moment with those around them. The atmosphere is impossible to ignore and if you see it simply as an inclusive celebration, it takes you in and fills your soul with good vibes and that is important to cherish.

INSPIRED BY BARACK OBAMA-TUPAC-NELSON MANDELA - MALCOLM X -
QUOTES OF: MICHAEL JORDAN - ROSA PARKS - MARTIN LUTHER KING JR -
BOOKER T WASHINGTON - MUHAMMAD ALI - MICHELLE OBAMA

UNDERGROUND

Service information

Date
Time **BLACK HISTORY**
            MONTH

@allontheboard

THE FUTURE BELONGS TO THOSE WHO
                        PREPARE FOR IT TODAY,
IF YOU FAIL OVER AND OVER AND OVER AGAIN
                    THERE'S ALWAYS ANOTHER WAY;
THE GREATEST GLORY IN LIVING IS RISING
                        EVERY TIME WE FALL,
EVERYBODY'S AT WAR WITH DIFFERENT THINGS,
            UNDERNEATH WE ARE THE SAME AFTER ALL.
MEASURE THE OBSTACLES WE OVERCOME WHILE
                    TRYING TO SUCCEED,
THE TIME IS ALWAYS RIGHT TO DO WHAT IS RIGHT
                    AND LOVE IS ALL WE NEED;
FROM THE EARTH TO ABOVE, STICK WITH LOVE,
            HATE IS TOO GREAT A BURDEN TO BEAR,
IT ISN'T THE MOUNTAIN THAT WEARS US DOWN,
            IT'S THE PEBBLE IN THE SHOES WE WEAR.
YOU NEVER KNOW HOW STRONG YOU ARE
                UNTIL BEING STRONG IS THE ONLY CHOICE,
SUCCESS ISN'T ABOUT HOW MUCH MONEY YOU MAKE,
                BUT, THE POWER IN YOUR TRUE VOICE;
NEVER BE FEARFUL ABOUT WHAT YOU ARE DOING,
            LIVE YOUR LIFE AS A MODEL FOR OTHERS,
DO NOT FEAR THE FUTURE, BE INVOLVED AND
                    HELP SHAPE IT,
    LET'S LIVE OUR LIVES AS SISTERS AND BROTHERS.

UNDERGROUND

Service information

Date COME ON

Time ENGLAND

LET NOT THE WEIGHT OF EXPECTATION FROM THIS
GLORIOUS NATION,
BECOME A HEAVY BURDEN UPON RIGID SHOULDERS;
SHAKE OFF THE SHACKLES OF FEAR AND STARE THE GODS OF IMMORTALITY,
DIRECTLY IN THEIR EYES WITH A FOCUSED CONCENTRATION.
NOW IS OUR TIME,
THIS IS OUR MOMENT TO SHINE,
AND TO STAND SIDE BY SIDE WITH THE MARBLED STATUES OF LEGENDS
SITUATED IN A GOLDEN PANTHEON OF GLORY.
FOR EVERY GOAL THAT IS SCORED, THE THREE LIONS WILL ROAR;
FOR EACH GOAL WE CONCEDE, THOSE LIONS WILL BLEED.
BLOOD, SWEAT AND TEARS ARE TEMPORARY
AND A SMALL PRICE TO PAY IN COMPARISON TO A LIFETIME OF REGRET.
ENGLAND IS DREAMING OF VICTORY FROM THE BEAUTIFUL GAME.
BE INSPIRED AND COME ALIVE WITH IMAGINATION;
AS A FRIENDLY WAR IS FOUGHT BETWEEN NATIONS,
IN A CARNIVAL OF COLOUR AND JOY;
LET THE BALL BE YOUR AMMUNITION,
AND YOUR FEET BE THE WEAPONS OF CHOICE.
LET US NOT DWELL ON UNFULFILLED PROMISES
OF GOLDEN GENERATIONS,
OR OF FOOTBALL COMING HOME.
DO IT FOR YOUR COUNTRY,
DO IT FOR YOURSELVES.
COME ON ENGLAND.

Service information

Date CONGRATULATIONS
Time HARRY & MEGHAN

CONGRATULATIONS HARRY AND MEGHAN ON YOUR BIG DAY,
YOU MAKE A HANDSOME GROOM AND A BEAUTIFUL BRIDE;
A NATION WILL CELEBRATE THE OCCASION AND THE WORLD WILL WATCH,
AS YOU TIE THE KNOT AND STAND SIDE BY SIDE.
EVERY GUEST WILL LOOK THEIR BEST AND BE DRESSED TO IMPRESS,
THERE MAY BE TEARS OF JOY AS MEGHAN WALKS DOWN THE AISLE;
EVEN IF YOU FLUFF YOUR LINES, THINGS WILL BE FINE,
JUST SWAP RINGS, SAY "I DO", THEN KISS AND SMILE.
THE PHOTOGRAPHERS WILL SNAP AWAY, AS THE BRIDE
                                        THROWS HER BOUQUET,
TO CATCH IT, WOMEN HAVE TO BE AGILE AND QUICK;
WHAT CAN YOU GET A ROYAL COUPLE FOR A WEDDING PRESENT?
A GOLD PLATED TOASTER OR A SILVER SELFIE STICK.
THE GROOM MAY BE NERVOUS ABOUT HIS BROTHER'S 'BEST MAN' SPEECH,
BUT, IT WILL MAKE THE GUESTS GRIN AND BE A WINNER;
GLASSES WILL BE RAISED FOR THIS AMAZING DAY,
THEN THE NEWLYWEDS WILL CUT THE CAKE AFTER THEIR DINNER.
ICONS OF MUSIC WILL PERFORM AT THE EVENING RECEPTION,
WILL IT BE ADELE, ED SHEERAN, THE SPICE GIRLS OR RIGHT SAID FRED;
NATURALLY THE QUEEN WILL DANCE TO ABBA AND
                PRINCE CHARLES WILL DAD DANCE TO STORMZY,
WITH A CHEEKY LITTLE 'OOPS UPSIDE ONE'S HEAD'.

@allontheboard

Service information

Date CONGRATULATIONS
Time WILLIAM & KATE

CONGRATULATIONS WILLIAM AND KATE, FOR THE BIRTH
OF PRINCE LOUIS
A ROYAL BUNDLE OF JOY AND A LITTLE JEWEL IN THE CROWN;
HARRY AND MEGHAN CAN PERFORM BABYSITTING DUTIES,
IF YOU BOTH FANCY A NIGHT OUT ON THE TOWN.

BABIES ARE ADORABLE AND ALSO A BEAUTIFUL BLESSING,
WHEN THEY SMILE YOU FEEL TALLER THAN THE SHARD;
BUT, IT CAN CAUSE STRESS, WHEN THEY ARE MAKING A MESS,
AND THEIR NAPPIES NEED MORE CHANGING THAN THE GUARD.

A BABY DOESN'T CARE IF YOU'RE THE FUTURE KING AND QUEEN,
WHEN THEY ARRIVE IN YOUR WORLD, THEY BECOME THE BOSS;
THEY WILL LET YOU KNOW WHEN THEY ARE HUNGRY,
OR IF THEY NEED BURPING,
THEY GUARANTEE YOU CUDDLES AND SLEEP LOSS.
TODAY SOCIAL MEDIA WILL GO CRAZY, THE EYES OF
THE WORLD WILL BE WATCHING,
THIS WONDERFUL NEWS WILL BE THE TALK OF PLANET EARTH;
CONGRATULATIONS TO ALL THE FAMILIES,
WELCOMING NEW ARRIVALS,
AND TO ALL THE MUM'S IN THIS WORLD GIVING BIRTH.

@allontheboard

Service information

Date

Time <u>EID MUBARAK</u>

MAY EVERY STEP OF YOUR JOURNEY THROUGH LIFE BE BLESSED,

MAY JOY AND HAPPINESS COME YOUR WAY;

MAY YOUR HEARTS BE FILLED BY LOVE

AND YOUR MINDS FILLED WITH WISDOM,

AS YOU CELEBRATE TODAY.

LET'S BE KIND TO EACH OTHER, BE THERE FOR ONE ANOTHER,

LIVE OUR LIVES IN PEACE WITH LOVE AND HARMONY;

EID MUBARAK TO EVERYONE CELEBRATING IN THE WORLD,

ETERNAL BLESSINGS TO OUR MUSLIM FRIENDS AND FAMILY.

@allontheboard

Service information

Date **WEAR THE ROSE**

Time ENGLAND'S RUGBY WORLD CUP SQUAD

by
@allontheboard

VICTORY IS THE PRIZE, PAIN IS THE PRICE,

TRUE CHAMPIONS AREN'T ALWAYS THE ONES THAT WIN;

AS YOU GET FURTHER THE BELIEF GROWS INSIDE,

WE WILL CHEER YOU ON, WEAR THE ROSE WITH PRIDE,

TOGETHER EVERYONE ACHIEVES MORE WHEN THEY

NEVER GIVE IN.

SCARS AND INJURIES HEAL, GLORY LASTS FOREVER,

RUGBY IS A WAY OF LIFE AND IMPOSSIBLE TO FORGET;

IT DOESN'T MATTER IF YOU WIN BY AN INCH

OR WIN BY A MILE,

WINNING IS WINNING, THE ONLY PAIN IS REGRET.

@allontheboard

Service information

Date
Time EXAM RESULTS

OBVIOUSLY YOU'RE FEELING NERVOUS AND YOU DON'T DESERVE THIS,
THE WAITING HAS CAUSED SO MUCH STRESS,
DON'T LET GRADES DECIDE YOUR FATE, IT'S NEVER TOO LATE,
WHATEVER YOU GET YOU CAN STILL BE A SUCCESS.

AS YOU WAIT FOR YOUR LETTERS CONTAINING NUMBERS OR LETTERS,
TELLING YOU HOW WELL YOU HAVE DONE;
IF YOU ARE DISAPPOINTED WITH YOUR RESULTS, DON'T FEEL IT'S ALL OVER,
YOUR LIFE HAS ONLY JUST BEGUN.

WE WISH YOU ALL THE BEST, IT'S HARD NOT TO GET STRESSED,
DON'T LET EXAM RESULTS AFFECT YOUR MENTAL HEALTH;
WE BELIEVE IN YOU AND OTHERS DO TOO,
HOLD YOUR HEAD UP HIGH AND BELIEVE IN YOURSELF.

IN TIME YOU WILL REALISE THAT THERE IS MORE TO LIFE,
THAN THE LETTERS INSIDE THE ENVELOPE;
DON'T STOP DREAMING, ALWAYS BELIEVE,
KEEP THE FAITH AND NEVER LOSE HOPE.

@allontheboard

Service information

Date HAPPY FATHERS

Time DAY

THANKS FOR BEING A FANTASTIC DAD,
AND FOR EVERYTHING YOU DO;
THANKS FOR BEING THE FIRST SUPERHERO,
THAT I EVER KNEW.
THANKS FOR YOUR REASSURING HUGS,
AND TELLING ME IT'S ALRIGHT;
THANKS FOR THE BEDTIME STORIES,
WHEN YOU TUCKED ME IN AT NIGHT.
THANKS FOR TEACHING ME HANDY TIPS,
AND ALL OF THE WORDS OF ADVICE;
THANKS FOR ALWAYS FORGIVING ME,
WHEN MY BEHAVIOUR WASN'T SO NICE.
THANKS FOR PUTTING A ROOF OVER MY HEAD,
AND FOR WORKING TO PAY THE BILLS;
THANKS FOR YOUR CHRISTMAS CRACKER STYLE JOKES,
AND SHOWING OFF WITH YOUR DIY SKILLS.
THANKS FOR THE HELP WITH MY HOMEWORK,
AND HELPING ME TO PREPARE FOR EACH TEST;
THANKS FOR TREATING MUM LIKE A QUEEN,
AND POINTING OUT SHE ALWAYS KNOWS BEST.
THANKS FOR YOUR DANCE MOVES AT PARTIES,
LIKE JOHN TRAVOLTA, BUT, SLIGHTLY LESS HIP;
THANKS FOR BEING OBLIVIOUS TO HOW LOUD YOU SNORE,
AND BLAMING THE DOG WHEN YOU LET ONE RIP.

@allontheboard

Service information

Date **WIMBLEDON**

Time

IT'S THAT SPECIAL TIME OF YEAR AGAIN,
WHEN THOUSANDS OF US PURCHASE A RACKET;
THE STRAWBERRIES AND CREAM TASTE JUST LIKE A DREAM,
BUT, SOMETIMES COST A PACKET.
WIMBLEDON IS PRETTY, IT'S SCENIC AND SO GREEN,
SO TAKE A LOOK AROUND AND SNIFF A FLOWER;
WOULDN'T IT BE COOL, TO CATCH A TENNIS BALL,
AS AN ACE IS SERVED AT 100 MILES PER HOUR?
WE SHALL DO A SUNDANCE IF THERE IS A CHANCE,
TO GET RID OF THE RAIN CLOUDS ABOVE;
A GREAT SET GIVES US TINGLES, SO LET THE SINGLES MINGLE,
TO FIND THIRTY OR FORTY LOVE.
NOTHING COMES UP TO SCRATCH LIKE AN EPIC MATCH,
BEING PLAYED ON THE CENTRE COURT;
PLEASE ASK THE STAFF WHERE THE NEAREST TOILETS ARE,
IF YOU FEEL LIKE YOU MAY GET CAUGHT SHORT,
WE SHALL KEEP YOU SAFE AND SOUND, ON THE UNDERGROUND,
AND HELP YOU GET FROM A TO B;
WHEN THE KINGS AND QUEENS ARE CROWNED, THERE WILL BE
CHEERS FROM MURRAY MOUND AND SMILES ON THE BBC.
SO CHEER ON THE LEGENDS, AS THEY QUESTION DECISIONS,
WITH GROUNDSTROKES, VOLLEYS AND LOBS;
OUR STAFF CAN SHOW YOU THE WAY AND GET YOU HOME SAFE,
THEY ARE EVER SO GOOD AT THEIR JOBS.

@allontheboard

Service information

Date HAPPY

Time HALLOWEEN

BY ALLONTHEBOARD

IT'S THAT TIME OF YEAR AGAIN, IT WILL BE SUCH A <u>SCREAM</u>
WHEN YOU CAN DRESS UP AS <u>PENNYWISE</u> WITH A RED BALLOON
AND HAUNT A <u>FREDDY KRUEGER</u> DREAM.
<u>STRANGER THINGS</u> MAY MAKE YOU JUMP, WITH PUMPKINS AND
BUMPS IN THE NIGHT;
WEREWOLVES CAN LET THEIR HAIR DOWN,
AND <u>VAMPIRES</u> CAN GO OUT FOR A BITE.
WALK LIKE A ZOMBIE, WRAP UP LIKE <u>THE MUMMY</u>
OR BE WHATEVER YOU LIKE;
IF YOU'RE FEELING FLASH, YOU CAN SPLASH THE CASH AND
DRESS UP AS JIGSAW ON HIS LITTLE BIKE.
SPIDERWEBS ON WALLS, <u>GOBLINS AND GHOULS</u>,
CLEAN UP WITH A WITCH'S BROOMSTICK;
DON'T EAT TOO MANY SWEETS WHEN YOU <u>TRICK OR TREAT</u>,
OR YOU MAY END UP BEING SICK.
DON'T FEAR THE WALKING DEAD, OR A GHOST
THAT LOOKS LIKE A BED SHEET;
BE CREEPY, KOOKY AND A LITTLE BIT SPOOKY,
DO <u>THE MONSTER MASH</u> AND TRICK OR TREAT.

@allontheboard

Service information

Date HAPPY CHINESE
Time   NEW YEAR

HAPPY CHINESE NEW YEAR TO ALMOST A QUARTER OF THE WORLD
                                    CELEBRATING IT,
MAY IT BLESS YOU AND YOU EMBRACE WHAT IT BRINGS
                                        INTO YOUR HEARTS;
IT'S ALSO KNOWN AS 'CHUNJIE' AND THE SPRING FESTIVAL,
PLANTING AND HARVESTING WITH NEW BEGINNINGS AND FRESH STARTS

IT IS A DAY FOR PRAYING TO GODS AND FIGHTING OFF MONSTERS,
SCARING THEM WITH FIRECRACKERS
                AND LOSING BAD LUCK, NEGATIVITY AND FEAR;
BEAUTIFUL FIREWORKS ARE SET OFF TO LIGHT UP A BRILLIANT NIGHT,
THE MORNING WELCOMES YOU WITH GOOD LUCK AND
                                    A BRAND NEW YEAR.

IN RED ENVELOPES CHILDREN RECEIVE LUCKY MONEY,
                IT'S IMPORTANT TO REUNITE THE FAMILY,
WITH PLENTY OF DUMPLINGS AND FANTASTIC DECORATIONS;
ON NEW YEAR'S DAY DON'T SWEEP UP OR
                THROW OUT ANY THIS OR ANY THAT,
THE CELEBRATIONS WILL END WITH PARTYING
            AND LANTERNS CAUSING AMAZING ILLUMINATIONS.

@allontheboard

Service information

Date EACH FOR
Time EQUAL

<u>INTERNATIONAL WOMEN'S DAY</u>

by
@allontheboard

UNITY AND SHARED RESPONSIBILITY ARE THE KEY
TO DRIVING THE WORLD TO TRUE GENDER EQUALITY AND HARMONY,
IT'S NOT JUST FOR ONE DAY, IT SHOULD ALWAYS BE THIS WAY;
TOGETHER WE CAN HELP TO CREATE A GENDER EQUAL WORLD,
WE ARE ALL PARTS OF THE WHOLE,
WE CAN MAKE CHANGE HAPPEN WITH OUR INDIVIDUAL ACTIONS,
THE THOUGHTS WE THINK, OUR BEHAVIOUR AND WHAT WE SAY.
BROADEN PERCEPTIONS, CHALLENGE STEREOTYPES, FIGHT BIAS
AND IMPROVE
SITUATIONS.
GENDER EQUALITY IS ESSENTIAL FOR HUMANITY TO THRIVE;
CELEBRATE WOMEN'S ACHIEVEMENTS BY HAVING
GENDER EQUALITY IN EVERY BOARDROOM,
EVERY WORKPLACE AND EVERY GOVERNMENT,
LET'S ALL BE EACH FOR EQUAL,
WE TRULY NEED ONE ANOTHER TO SURVIVE.

@allontheboard

UNDERGROUND

Service information

Date

Time **MOTHER'S DAY**

<u>THANK YOU MUM</u>

THANKS FOR BEING A WONDERFUL MUM AND EVERYTHING YOU DO,
THANKS FOR ALL THE GOOD TIMES AND THANKS FOR BEING YOU;
THANKS FOR FILLING MY WORLD WITH LOVE AND EVERY SINGLE MEMORY,
THANKS FOR EVERY MEAL YOU'VE EVER MADE AND EVERY CUP OF TEA.
THANKS FOR HAVING SUPERGLUE, EVERY TIME MY HEART MIGHT BREAK,
THANKS FOR YOUR TIME AND PATIENCE AND FORGIVING MY MISTAKES;
THANKS FOR BEING FUNNY, SO CARING AND SO WARM,
THANK YOU FOR PROTECTING ME WITH SHELTER FROM ANY STORM.
THANKS FOR BEING BEAUTIFUL, SO SWEET AND SO DIVINE,
THANKS FOR MAKING ME SO PROUD OF KNOWING THAT YOU'RE MINE;
THANK YOU FOR INSPIRING ME TO FOLLOW ALL OF MY DREAMS,
THANKS FOR ALWAYS SHOWING ME NOTHING IS AS BAD AS IT SEEMS;
THANKS FOR BEING A WARRIOR AND NOT GIVING IN TO YOUR PAIN,
THANKS FOR MAKING A CRAZY WORLD SEEM INCREDIBLY SANE.
THANK YOU FOR YOUR INNER STRENGTH AND MAKING THE DARKNESS BRIGHT,
THANK YOU FOR ALWAYS FIXING THINGS AND MAKING IT ALRIGHT;
THANKS FOR THE PAST AND THE PRESENT, THE FUTURE AND ETERNITY,
THANKS FOR MAKING ME FEEL BLESSED AND GRATEFUL TO BE ME.

@allontheboard

Service information

Date

Time **PRIDE**

by @allontheboard

HAVING AN OPEN MIND AND AN OPEN HEART
IS A GOOD PLACE TO START,
WHEN EVERYONE IS TREATED AS EQUALS, WE ARE MORE FREE;
THIS WORLD WOULD BE BETTER IF WE MADE AN EFFORT
TO BE MORE UNDERSTANDING,
BE PROUD, LOVE IS LOUD, SO LET EVERYONE SEE.
WHEN PEOPLE SEE YOU STAND UP FOR YOUR RIGHTS,
MAY OTHERS STAND UP WITH YOU;
DON'T BE AFRAID TO BE HONEST ABOUT WHO YOU ARE,
AND TO YOURSELF ALWAYS BE TRUE.

LOVE IS LOVE AND IT HAS NO GENDER, SO LET'S NOT PRETEND,
THAT BEING DIFFERENT IS A LIFESTYLE CHOICE;
THOSE WHO HAVE NO ACCEPTANCE ARE THE ONES
WITH THE PROBLEMS,
EXPRESS YOURSELF AND USE THE POWER OF YOUR VOICE.
CELEBRATE THE DIVERSITY OF HUMANITY,
AND TOGETHER LET'S MARCH SIDE BY SIDE;
BE WHO YOU ARE, DON'T BE SCARED OF COMING OUT,
TASTE THE RAINBOW AND STAND TALL WITH PRIDE.

@allontheboard

Service information

Date **HAPPY**

Time **ST PATRICK'S DAY**

FROM CANADA TO DOVER, AND ALL THE WORLD OVER;
EVERYONE WOULD LOVE TO FIND, A LUCKY FOUR LEAF CLOVER.
MAY EVERY RAINBOW YOU CHASE, BE BLESSED WITH A POT OF GOLD;
IF YOU HAVE ONE DRINK TOO MANY,
                FIND A LAMP POST OR A GOOD FRIEND TO HOLD.
FROM DYEING THE RIVER GREEN IN CHICAGO,
                AND THE PARADES IN BOSTON AND NEW YORK;
TO LONDON AND DUBLIN, THE EXCITEMENT WILL BE BUBBLING,
                SO HAVE A DRINK, HAVE A DANCE AND A TALK.
RAISE A GLASS AND A SMILE TO THE EMERALD ISLE,
                THE SHAMROCK AND THE HOLY TRINITY;
MAY YOU ALL HAVE HOPE, FAITH, LOVE AND LUCK,
                WHEREVER IN THIS WORLD THAT YOU MAY BE.
DRESS AS A LEPRECHAUN OR BE SEEN IN GREEN,
                AND MAY THE 'LUCK OF THE IRISH' COME YOUR WAY;
EMBRACE THE WORLD IN YOUR ARMS,
                HAVE FUN WITH YOUR LUCKY CHARMS,
AND TO BE SURE TO HAVE A <u>HAPPY ST. PATRICK'S DAY.</u>

@allontheboard

Service information

Date

Time

ORDINARY BOWL

SUPER BOWL

@allontheboard

Service information

Date HAPPY

Time THANKSGIVING DAY

(TO OUR FAMILY AND FRIENDS IN THE U.S.A)

THIS IS WHAT <u>WE'RE</u> THANKFUL FOR . . .

TECHNOLOGY THAT MAKES DISTANT LOVED ONES EASY TO REACH,
PEOPLE WILLING TO TEACH AND THE FREEDOM OF SPEECH;
THE BEAUTY OF NATURE, RAINBOWS, MOUNTAINS AND SUNSETS,
THE LAUGHTER OF CHILDREN AND THE COMPANY OF PETS.
EXPERIENCING HIGHS AFTER LOWS AND LEARNING FROM MISTAKES,
MUSIC, BOOKS, ART AND MOVIES, DANCING, DOUGHNUTS AND BIRTHDAY CAKES;
BRAINS THAT THINK, CLEAN WATER TO DRINK, MEMORIES INSIDE THE MIND,
GOOD FRIENDS TO DEPEND ON, PARTNERS TO LEAN ON

AND WHEN STRANGERS ARE BEING KIND.
DIVERSITY, SECURITY, ELECTRICITY AND AN ABILITY TO READ,
IN ANY SITUATION, AN EDUCATION AND MEDICATION WE NEED;
PROTECTION FROM A STORM, CLOTHES TO KEEP US WARM,

WISDOM THAT COMES WITH AGE,
FRESH AIR TO BREATHE, DREAMS TO BELIEVE, USING THE WORLD AS A STAGE.
BEDS TO SLEEP IN, INNOVATORS INVENTING,

THE SUN, MOON AND STARS UP ABOVE,
BEING YOURSELF AND WHATEVER YOUR HEALTH,
HAVING PARENTS OR FAMILY TO LOVE;
HAVE A WONDERFUL THANKSGIVING, WHICHEVER STATE YOU LIVE IN,

FROM CALIFORNIA TO NEW YORK,
MAY YOU HAVE PLENTY OF FOOD WITH THOSE WHO YOU LOVE

AND ALSO THE TIME TO TALK.

@allontheboard

Service information

Date

Time

THERE WILL ALWAYS BE MUSICIANS WHO HAVE HAD A CHEEKY DRINK OR TWO,
AND GUEST PRESENTERS STRUGGLING TO READ THE AUTO CUE;
LEGENDS GETTING CUT OFF ACCEPTING AN AWARD AND FLIPPING BIRDS,
EDITORS WORKING SO QUICKLY ON THE LIVE SHOW TO BLEEP OUT ANY SWEAR WORDS.

THERE'S ONLY ONE DIRECTION TO GO IF YOU'RE LIKE HARRY STYLES AND YOU GET
CAUGHT SHORT,
IF NOMINEES DON'T WIN THEIR CATEGORIES IT'S ALWAYS BEST TO BE A GOOD SPORT;
GOD BLESS THE QUEEN OF POP WHO TOOK AN UNFORTUNATE DROP UPON THE STAIRS,
JARVIS COCKER, POP STARS, RAPPERS AND ROCKERS SHAKING THEIR DERRIERES.

MICS BEING DROPPED AFTER AN ACCEPTANCE SPEECH IS SIMPLY ROCK AND ROLL,
ICONIC MOMENTS, POLITICAL STATEMENTS AND A LITTLE CONTROVERSY MAKE SURE
THE NIGHT IS NEVER DULL;
STUNNING PERFORMANCES FROM STARS WHO HAVE OWNED IT LIKE ADELE WITH
'SOMEONE LIKE YOU,'
THE AWARDS SHOW STARTED OFF AT WEMBLEY AND HAS ENDED UP AT THE O2.

FROM STORMZY WHIPPING UP A STORM TO THE SPICE GIRLS WITH
'WHO DO YOU THINK YOU ARE?'
IN A UNION JACK DRESS OR ACCOMPANIED BY PUPPETS
EVERY PERFORMER ON STAGE HAS SHONE LIKE A STAR;
EVERY WINNER AND NOMINEE HAS MADE THEIR OWN OUTSTANDING CONTRIBUTION
TO MUSIC,
THERE HAS BEEN RIVALRY AND REVELRY AND SO MANY HITS;
THANKS FOR ALL THE MEMORIES, HAPPY 40TH SHOW TO THE BRITS.

@allontheboard

Service information

Date HAPPY BIRTHDAY

Time HER MAJESTY
THE QUEEN

by
@allontheboard

HAPPY 93ʀᴅ BIRTHDAY YOUR MAJESTY,
MAY ALL YOUR DREAMS AND WISHES COME TRUE;
TROOPING THE COLOUR WILL BE FOR YOUR
                     OTHER BIRTHDAY IN THE SUMMER,
YOU'RE SO LOVELY AND IT'S NICE THAT YOU HAVE TWO.

LET THIS YEAR NOT BE `HORRIBILIS`,
                 MAY IT BE AN `ANNUS` TREMENDOUS,
MAKE SOME JOURNEYS WITH YOUR FREEDOM PASS
                 AND TRAVEL THROUGH THE ZONES;
A CHEEKY PARTY AT THE PALACE WOULDN'T
                     WAKE UP ANY NEIGHBOURS,
ROYAL MUSICAL CHAIRS IS JUST A GAME OF THRONES.

SLIGHTLY LONGER IT MAY TAKE
          TO BLOW OUT THE CANDLES ON YOUR CAKE,
WE SEND YOU LOVE AND WISH YOU THE BEST OF HEALTH;
ONE THING THAT WE DO WONDER
                     IS WHEN YOU REACH 100,
WILL YOU SEND A TELEGRAM TO ONESELF?

LOVE @allontheboard

Service information

Date

Time

The nation is so excited about
the new arrival coming soon
for one of the world's most
favourite couples.
She is so beautiful, with a
smile that could light up any room
and we know she is so happy with
her red headed, cheeky Prince Charming.
It won't be long now
Stacey Solomon and Joe Swash.

We are also excited about
Meghan and Harry's baby announcement
coming very soon. Love @allontheboard

Service information

Date

Time

Merry Christmas to every one of
        our followers around the World.
Thank you for following us and
                    thanks for being you.
We really do appreciate it and
                it means the World to us.
We hope you have a wonderful festive period
        and may your dreams and wishes
                come true in 2020.
If you don't celebrate Christmas
        We wish you love and peace too.

        Love
                @allontheboard

I was born in London in a hospital very near to London Bridge. Yeah, you know London Bridge. It's not that fancy bridge that shows off by opening up whenever big boats go sailing past it on the River Thames. It's the one that does exactly what it says on the tin. It's a bridge. It does what bridges do. Despite what a certain song accuses it of, it is definitely not falling down.

Maybe it's because I'm a Londoner, but I absolutely love London Town: the history, the scenery, the buildings, the culture and the people. We go through good times, we go through bad times; there are times when we are divided and times when we are united. But, we are always London.

EI and myself work as station assistants all over the Tube network and have worked at over 100 stations across London. It's amazing the sights you get to see and the wonderful people that you meet and talk to from all over the world. Sometimes you see celebrities using the Tube as well. Don't be too surprised if you're on a train one day and Rihanna or Paul McCartney are sitting on the seat next to you.

There are many, many beautiful places and cities all over the world, but there is nowhere quite like London. If you are from London or have visited London, then you will know what we are talking about. If you have never been to London, come over when you get the chance. We will have a cup of tea ready and waiting for you.

London is truly a marvellous place full of history, stunning architecture and plenty of beautiful sights. There is no other skyline quite like the skyline of London.

We do give our buildings funny names though. The Gherkin? The Walkie Talkie?

I have lived in London my whole life and I love calling it my home.

Whenever I give directions to tourists and recommendations for places to visit I feel so proud talking about London and all of the sights they can see and places that they can go to.

You don't have to be born in London to be a Londoner. It's a state of mind and a way of life. Anybody can be a Londoner.

We are London.

I love London. I was born here and have lived here all of my life. Sure, it has its ups and its downs. No city is perfect, but its intricacies and, most importantly, its people are the spring that keeps bouncing the best things above the rest.

There is history, there is culture, and there is fun to be had in so many different ways. The traditional and modern elements of the most famous landmarks and heritage offer themselves to celebration and humour, and we certainly enjoy highlighting those for the benefit of all, but we also love to honour the everyday things that make it tick.

N1 and I work on the London Underground, as you know, but unlike other staff you may be accustomed to seeing in your usual station, we work in any station across the network when required. We have operated in well over 100 stations each, sometimes at a different station every day of our week. We know the Tube extremely well, and it does mean you'd have to be Sherlock to find us.

Our job offers us a chance to see people from all walks of life every single day, flowing through the stations towards the places where the city needs them in order to thrive. We have spoken to so many people because of this job, with characters from quite possibly every country there is, every religion (even the Jedi), and every possible job.

I've seen crowds partying towards the Notting Hill Carnival with an energy unlike anything you can imagine. (Okay, maybe a volcano has as much energy but it's close.) I've seen people create art as performers, musicians or painters. I've seen couples fall in love on a platform, and some of the most spontaneous moments of care and consideration. This city has everything, and it's thanks to all of us who shape it.

Over the years our work has been shared across the globe and it is truly special to know that so many people from so many different countries can connect with what we write, regardless of language barriers or those words being in a digital space. However, in London people interact with the actual boards. It means we can reach people in real life and break through the mundane elements of their day by giving them a slice of delight they weren't expecting.

This chapter is about celebrating the things I love about our city, and that I find inspiring or funny. It's filled with peak wordplay, if I don't say so myself, and most importantly it's about my home.

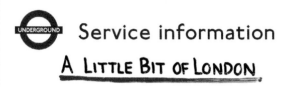

Service information

A LITTLE BIT OF LONDON

FROM THE SWINGING SIXTIES IN
CARNABY STREET,
TO BRITPOP IN CAMDEN AND EAST LONDON GRIME;
SEE THE WATERLOO SUNSET OR STROLL DOWN THE THAMES,
WHERE BIG BEN ALWAYS HAS TIME.
SO MANY SITES TO TAKE PHOTOS OF,
PALACES AND BUILDINGS SO TALL;
TAKE A CHEEKY SELFIE UPON TOWER BRIDGE,
OR IN FRONT OF THE ROYAL ALBERT HALL.
THE WEST END IS THE PLACE TO GO,
IF YOU WANT TO SEE A SHOW,
AND THERE ARE PREMIERES IN LEICESTER SQUARE;
IF YOU WANT TO SHOP UNTIL YOU DROP,
THERE ARE SO MANY STOPS,
AND SO MANY WAYS TO GET THERE.
THERE IS NO PLACE COOLER WHEN
IT GETS DARK, SEE WHERE TIME
BEGINS AT GREENWICH PARK,
WE ALWAYS SEEM TO TALK ABOUT THE WEATHER;
THIS CITY IS DIVERSE,
FOR BETTER AND FOR WORSE,
WE STAY STRONG AND WE
ALWAYS STAND TOGETHER.

@allontheboard

Service information

Date **A RIHANNA**

Time **LONDON GUIDE**

by @allontheboard

LONDON WE <u>LOVE THE WAY YOU LIE</u>
              BETWEEN THE UNDERGROUND AND THE SKY,
IN A LIST OF CITIES WITH HISTORY <u>YOU DA ONE</u>,
          SO, PLEASE <u>TAKE A BOW</u>;
THE U.K. WEATHER IS LIKE <u>RUSSIAN ROULETTE</u>,
      IF YOU HAVE NO <u>UMBRELLA</u> YOU'RE GONNA GET WET.
<u>WHERE HAVE YOU BEEN</u> IF YOU'VE NEVER BEEN TO LONDON,
          YOU SHOULD VISIT NOW.
TAXI DRIVERS LOVE TO CHAT AND ASK, "<u>WHAT'S MY NAME?</u>"
PLEASE DON'T BE A <u>RUDE BOY</u> OR A RUDE GIRL
         BY SAYING "<u>SHUT UP AND DRIVE</u>";
IF YOU MISS YOUR TRAIN DON'T FEEL LIKE
      A <u>MAN DOWN</u> IN CHINA TOWN OR
      THE <u>ONLY GIRL</u> IN S&MBANKMENT,
IN <u>FOURFIVESECONDS</u>, THE NEXT ONE WILL ARRIVE.
<u>DON'T STOP THE MUSIC</u> THE BUSKERS PLAY, THEY MAY SING
      A SONG THAT STAYS IN YOUR HEAD ALL DAY,
THE PEOPLE IN LONDON ARE ALL <u>DIAMONDS</u> AND EVER SO PRETTY,
RUSH HOUR CAN BE BERSERK WITH PEOPLE GOING
       TO <u>WORK</u>. WORK, WORK,
BUT, WHEN PUSH COMES TO SHOVE <u>WE FOUND LOVE</u> WITH
      THE WORLDS GREATEST CITY.

@allontheboard

Service information

Date **A SUPERHERO**
Time _____ TUBE GUIDE

EVERYONE IS WELCOME TO USE THE TUBE,
FROM <u>WONDER WOMAN</u> TO <u>BLACK PANTHER</u>;
YOU COULD BE <u>SPIDERMAN</u>, <u>BATMAN</u> OR <u>CAPTAIN</u> AMERICA,
BIG DAVE OR NEXT DOOR'S SAMANTHA.
IF YOUR MOBILITY IS IMPAIRED, YOU HAVE CHILDREN WITH YOU,
OR YOUR LUGGAGE IS A HUGE BULK;
USE THE BIG GATE PROVIDED AND DON'T BE THE <u>JOKER</u>
OR GET ANGRY LIKE <u>THE INCREDIBLE HULK.</u>
YOU MAY BE STRONG LIKE <u>THOR</u>, BUT IT MAY LEAVE YOU SORE,
SO, PLEASE DON'T OBSTRUCT ANY DOOR;
LET'S WORK AS A TEAM AND <u>MARVEL</u> AT OUR DREAM,
AND BE BETTER THAN <u>THE FANTASTIC FOUR.</u>
OUR MACHINES ARE ADVANCED LIKE THE SUIT OF <u>IRON MAN</u>,
THEY TAKE BANK CARDS, COINS AND CASH;
THE TUBE IS PRETTY QUICK, AS IT TRAVELS THROUGH LONDON,
BUT, NOT QUITE AS QUICK AS THE <u>FLASH</u>.
WE TRY TO KEEP OUR STATIONS CLEAN LIKE THE CLAWS OF
<u>WOLVERINE</u>,
AND IF YOU FEEL UNWELL, WE CAN GET YOU <u>DOCTOR STRANGE</u>;
FROM A TO B, OR <u>DC</u>, THE STAFF CAN MAKE IT EASY,
AND ADVISE <u>SUPERMAN</u> ON THE BEST PLACE HE COULD CHANGE.

@allontheboard

Service information

Date **EVERYONE NEEDS**

Time **A HOME**

EVERYONE SHOULD HAVE FOOD, WARMTH AND WATER,
AND A ROOF OVER THEIR HEAD;
NOBODY SHOULD BE SLEEPING ON COLD PAVING STONES,
USING BROKEN CARDBOARD BOXES FOR BEDS.
ANY ONE OF US COULD BE IN THAT SITUATION,
WITH FATE, BAD LUCK OR A WRONG DECISION;
CONFINED TO UNCERTAINTY WITHOUT 4 WALLS,
AND THE OUTSIDE WORLD BECOMES A PRISON.
EVERYBODY NEEDS HELP, EVERYBODY NEEDS ADVICE,
EVERYBODY NEEDS SOMEWHERE TO LIVE;
INSTEAD OF SPARE CHANGE, YOU COULD GIVE THEM FOOD,
AND THERE'S OTHER THINGS YOU CAN GIVE.
GIVE THEM SLEEPING BAGS, HOT DRINKS, TOILETRIES,
CLOTHES AND SOCKS,
AND A SPARE MOMENT OF YOUR TIME;
EVERY HOMELESS PERSON YOU SEE IS A HUMAN AND STARTED LIFE AS A BABY,
LOSING THE WAY WAS THEIR BIGGEST CRIME.
LIFE IS A HELTER SKELTER FOR THE POOR SOULS THAT HAVE NO SHELTER,
PLEASE DON'T IGNORE THEM AND PRETEND THEY ARE NOT THERE;
THEY DON'T NEED DRUGS OR ALCOHOL TO ESCAPE EXISTENCE,
THEY NEED OUR COMPASSION AND TO SHOW THEM THAT WE CARE.
EVERY ADULT, EVERY CHILD AND EVERY ANIMAL IN THE WORLD,
NEEDS A FUTURE AND A HOME THEY CAN AFFORD;
FROM HER MAJESTY THE QUEEN TO A STREETWISE TEEN,
LET'S HELP THE CRISIS AND ALL GET ON BOARD.

@allontheboard

Service information

Happy 40ᵗʰ Birthday
          Jubilee Line,
May your dreams come true;
Some say you're silver,
          Some say grey,
But, whatever you are,
          you're not blue.
You take fans to Wembley,
   The O2 Arena and West Ham,
You drop shoppers off
   at Stratford and Bond Street;
You show tourists Big Ben,
   Buckingham Palace and
      where Sherlock Holmes lived,
As lines go you're sorted
          and sweet.

   Love @allontheboard

Service information

Date **WEATHER**

Time **WARNING**

A Cockney Rhyming Special

CAN YOU ADAM AND EVE HOW PEAS IN THE POT
THE CURRANT BUN IS MAKING US FEEL?
IS IT HAVING A BUBBLE BATH?
WE DON'T WANT TO COMPLAIN, BUT WE WOULD LOVE
A BIT OF PLEASURE AND PAIN.
DON'T LET YOURSELF OR YOUR CHINA PLATES
GET INTO BARNEY RUBBLE OR A TWO AND EIGHT.
LOOK AFTER EACH OTHER.
AS YOU BALL AND CHALK DOWN THE FROG AND TOAD
IN YOUR DINKY DOOS, THINK OF HOW HOT THE GROUND
WILL BE FOR CAT'S AND DOG'S PAWS AS THE TEMPERATURE SOARS.
PLEASE DON'T DUCK AND DIVE WITH THE SUN CREAM.
APPLY IT TO YOUR BOAT RACE, YOUR FIREMAN'S HOSE,
YOUR CHALK FARMS AND ANY AREAS OF YOUR BODY
EXPOSED TO THE SUN.
MAKE SURE TO DRINK PLENTY OF WATER IN YOUR
NORTH AND SOUTH.
PLEASE READ THE BRASS TACKS ONLINE AND
FOLLOW ADVICE ON THE CUSTARD AND JELLY OR
THE RADIO ON HOW TO STAY COOL.

@allontheboard

Service information

Date **LONDON**

Time **FASHION WEEK**

IF YOU HAVE A PASSION FOR FASHION, BUT YOUR CASH HAS A RATION,
MAKE A BEELINE FOR THE A-LINE WITH YOUR CREDIT CARD;
FROM A MUST HAVE TO A TREND DU JOUR, BE COSMOPOLITAN AND MAKE IT YOURS,
IN STYLE AND ON-TREND WITH VINTAGE AND AVANT-GARDE.
TREAT YOUR MUM, DAD, SON OR DAUGHTER TO SOME BRAND NEW PRET-A-PORTER,
NEW YORK, PARIS, L.A., MILAN, WE WISH WE COULD BE THERE;
THIS WEEK LONDON IS THE PLACE TO BE, DRESS IN NYLON AND FLAUNT ID,
IT WOULD BE LUCKY TO MINGLE WITH STELLA, KATE, VICTORIA, AND VANITY FAIR.
JE NE SAIS QUOI WE JUDGE A BOOKER BY THEIR FIRST LOOKS,
AS WE'RE PERISCOPING THE RISER AND THE GLITTERATI;
DON'T BE SWAG SWIPED IN A SILHOUETTE, WEARING A BIAS CUT AND REGRET,
PLAYING PEEK-A-BOO WITH THE COMPLEX PAPARAZZI.
DON'T GET IN ANY TROUBLE, IF YOU TRY THE 3-TO-1 SHUFFLE,
WHEN THE MODELS VOGUE ON THE CATWALK, DON'T FORGET WHERE YOU ARE;
DREAM THE DREAM AND KEEP IT REAL, PULL A FACE LIKE ZOOLANDER'S BLUE STEEL,
IN MARIE CLAIRE, ELLE, GQ OR HARPER'S BAZAAR.
DON'T MESS WITH THE DRESSER OR THE CASTING DIRECTOR,
THERE'S NO NEED FOR HANDBAGS AT DAWN OR ANY TIARAS AND TEARS;
MAY YOU ENJOY THE RUN OF THE SHOW, FROM THE BACK TO THE FROW,
BE DAZED AND AMAZED BY THE CHEVRONS AND CHANDELIERS.

@allontheboard

Service information

Date LONDON
Time MARATHON

by
@allontheboard

IT'S THAT TIME OF THE YEAR AGAIN,
WHEN THOUSANDS OF PEOPLE RUN;
RAISING MONEY AND AWARENESS FOR CHARITIES,
AND LONDON COMES TOGETHER AS ONE.

THIS CITY OF OURS IS BEAUTIFUL,
THERE ARE SO MANY SIGHTS TO BE SEEN;
WHEN YOU RUN PAST BUCKINGHAM PALACE,
GIVE A CHEEKY LITTLE WAVE TO THE QUEEN.

THE EYES OF THE WORLD ARE UPON YOU,
AND IF YOU FEEL LIKE YOU'VE HIT A BRICK WALL;
PLEASE KNOW THAT YOU HAVE INSPIRED A NATION,
WE REALLY ARE SO PROUD OF YOU ALL.

WHEN IT'S ALL OVER, LOOK BACK AT YOUR REMARKABLE ACHIEVEMENTS,
WEAR YOUR MEDAL WITH PRIDE ON YOUR CHEST;
EVERY ONE OF YOU TAKING PART IS A REAL LIFE SUPERHERO,
ON MONDAY YOU ALL DESERVE A DAY OF REST.

Service information

NOT A...

Date **QUOTE** OF THE **DAY**

Time

'WELCOME TO OXFORD CIRCUS . . .
HERE YOU WILL FIND THE GREATEST MINDS IN
THE WORLD TEACHING VALUABLE KNOWLEDGE
WHILE JUGGLING AND EVEN PERFORMING
GYMNASTICS ON THE SIDE . . . NO LION TAMING
THOUGH, THANK YOU!
WE ALSO SOMETIMES BOAT RACE WITH OUR PALS
FROM CAMBRIDGE HEATH AROUND OUR GIANT TENT
IN THE THAMES.
THERE'S EVEN A COUPLE OF CLOWNS ABOUT BUT
THEY'VE GONE FOR A CHEEKY CUP OF TEA BEFORE
THEY GO SHOPPING FOR SHOES.'

     – J. R. R. TOLKIEN (1865)

   OR WAS IT BIG DAVE?
     IT WAS ONE OF THEM.

@allontheboard

Service information

Date ON THE TUBE WITH......
Time SIR PAUL McCARTNEY

'AS MUCH AS I LOVE TO <u>DRIVE MY CAR</u>
ON <u>THE LONG AND WINDING ROAD</u>, I AM A <u>DAYTRIPPER</u>
AND LIKE FEELING AS <u>FREE AS A BIRD</u> TO GO
<u>HERE, THERE & EVERYWHERE</u>.

YES, I KNOW THE TUBE WON'T TAKE ME <u>ACROSS THE UNIVERSE</u>
OR GET ME <u>BACK IN THE U.S.S.R</u>, BUT, WITH A <u>TICKET TO RIDE</u>
YOU CAN GO ON A <u>MAGICAL MYSTERY TOUR</u> OF LONDON.

<u>YESTERDAY</u> I WAS AT A STATION AND I NEEDED ASSISTANCE.
<u>I SAW HER STANDING THERE</u> AND SAID,
'<u>HEY JUDE</u>, CAN I HAVE SOME <u>HELP</u>!',

SHE REPLIED, '<u>ANY TIME AT ALL</u>',
WHEN I TOLD HER I HAD SOME CONUNDRUMS SHE SAID,
'<u>WE CAN WORK IT OUT</u>'.

I NOW KNOW THAT YOU DON'T HAVE TO GO TO
AN <u>OCTOPUS'S GARDEN</u> TO GET AN OYSTER CARD
AND <u>I SHOULD HAVE KNOWN BETTER</u> THAT
A WEEKLY TRAVELCARD DOESN'T LAST <u>EIGHT DAYS A WEEK</u>'

       – SIR PAUL McCARTNEY
       (OR MAYBE IT WASN'T)

@allontheboard

Service information

Date **FOR FANS OF**

Time **TOWER HILL**

HELLO LOVELY PEOPLE, IT'S SO NICE TO HAVE YOU HERE,
WELCOME TO TOWER HILL;
LONDON IS OPEN TO EVERYONE IN THIS WORLD
FROM CHINA TO BRAZIL.
WHEN YOU EXIT THIS TRAIN THERE ARE AMAZING VIEWS,
LIKE THE TOWER OF LONDON AND THE SHARD;
PLEASE SEE OUR STAFF IF YOU NEED SOME ADVICE
WITH DIRECTIONS OR YOUR OYSTER CARD.
BETWEEN 4:00 PM AND 8:00 PM THIS STATION GETS BUSY,
WITH COMMUTERS COMING HOME FROM WORKING;
THERE ARE SO MANY BUILDINGS TO TAKE PHOTOS OF,
THE CITY HALL, THE WALKIE TALKIE AND THE GHERKIN.
THIS AREA ROCKS, GO SEE ST. KATHERINE'S DOCKS,
OR GO ON THE JACK THE RIPPER TOUR;
PLATFORMS 1 AND 2 GO WEST, PLATFORM 3 GOES EAST,
AND FENCHURCH STREET STATION IS NEXT DOOR.
JUST AROUND THE CORNER YOU WILL FIND TOWER BRIDGE,
IT'S REALLY NOT THAT FAR;
IF YOU EXIT THE STATION, AND WALK PAST THE ROMAN WALL,
YOU WILL GET TO TOWER GATEWAY DLR.
IF YOU NEED A TOILET OR YOU NEED TO DRAW OUT MONEY,
PLEASE DON'T WORRY OR HAVE ANY FEAR;
THERE ARE PUBLIC TOILETS, JUST BEFORE THE TOWER,
AND YOU WILL FIND A CASH MACHINE RIGHT HERE.

@allontheboard

Service information

Date

Time

THE TUBE

THE TUBE HAS MANY LINES AND MANY STATIONS TOO,
THERE ARE STAFF WHO CAN ASSIST YOU FROM WALTHAMSTOW TO WATERLOO;
PLEASE LISTEN TO THEIR DIRECTIONS BECAUSE THEY KNOW THE QUICKEST WAY,
THEY ONLY WANT WHAT'S BEST FOR YOU AND TO HELP TO MAKE YOUR DAY.

THE TUBE IS THERE FOR EVERYONE, SO PLEASE DON'T EVER BE SCARED,
IF YOU'RE A COMMUTER, A TOURIST, OR VISIBILITY OR MOBILITY IMPAIRED;
IT'S THE FASTEST WAY THROUGH LONDON AND IT STOPS AT EVERY SIGHT,
WE CAN GET YOU HOME FROM NIGHT CLUBS ON A FRIDAY OR SATURDAY NIGHT.

DRINKING, SMOKING AND VAPING IS NOT PERMITTED, WE HOPE YOU UNDERSTAND,
PLEASE KEEP YOUR BELONGINGS WITH YOU AND VERY CLOSE TO HAND;
NO MATTER WHERE YOU'RE FROM, WE CAN SHOW YOU IT'S NOT HARD,
TO GET FROM A TO B THEN C AND HOW TO USE AN OYSTER OR A CONTACTLESS CARD.

MUSEUMS AT SOUTH KENSINGTON, BUCKINGHAM PALACE AT GREEN PARK, CINEMAS
IN LEICESTER SQUARE,
PLEASE 'MIND THE GAP', IF IT'S ON THE MAP WE WILL GLADLY TAKE YOU THERE;
SOMETIMES FOR HEALTH AND SAFETY WE MAY HOLD A CROWD,
IF THERE'S A STATION WITH A TUNNEL SOME BIKES WON'T BE ALLOWED.

THE TRAINS CAN GET SO BUSY DURING EVERYDAY COMMUTES,
PLEASE SEEK SOME ASSISTANCE ON ADVICE ON ANY STEP-FREE ROUTES;
SOMETIMES THERE MAY BE SOME DELAYS, SUSPENSIONS OR ENGINEERING WORKS,
PLEASE DON'T SCREAM OR SHOUT,
OUR STAFF ARE ONLY HUMANS AND WILL TRY TO HELP YOU OUT.

PLEASE DON'T EVER FEEL EMBARRASSED OR TOO SHY,
TO LET US KNOW IF YOU'RE FEELING UNWELL;
WITH LOVE FROM NI AND EI OF ALL ON THE BOARD
AND EVERYONE AT TFL.

@allontheboard

At the beginning of 2020 so many people were saying that this was going to be their year, and there seemed to be excitement and optimism in the air. It didn't last for very long.

In times of trouble and fear all we want to do is be with those who we love and to hold on to them, but at the same time we have to protect those we love by keeping our distance from them. Special occasions, from weddings to sporting events, have been postponed and cancelled all over the world. The things we enjoyed doing and places we enjoyed going to for an escape from real life, like cinemas, shops, restaurants and bars, were all shut down. Children weren't able to go to school. People weren't able to go to work. Families weren't able to see one another. Jobs, businesses and careers ended. And, most importantly and devastatingly, so many lives were lost too. Very few people alive today have witnessed anything like this before. It seems like a weird nightmare that we can't wake up from, or a disaster movie in which we have been cast.

We had to go to work during the pandemic. As station assistants for Transport for London, we are essential workers and had to help other key workers get to their places of work, from those who work in hospitals and care homes to shop staff. During that time, we have tried to keep spirits up by celebrating heroes, wishing people happy birthday, trying to look on the brighter side of life and reminding people that they are not alone. We placed our boards at stations in London during the pandemic, but technology has allowed us to share our messages with people all over the world.

It has been something that the whole world has had to deal with together, while for safety reasons keeping apart.

Many things in life and in this world of ours are out of our control, but we can control how we behave and how we treat other people. We should always treat people with kindness, even more so in these times.

If we have to get used to a new normal for a while, then so be it. What was the old normal? What is normal anyway? We shall get used to a new normal together. It's tough, but so are we. We can do this. If we all jump on board the same boat and keep rowing in the same direction we will get to where we are going. We will get stronger. Some days it feels like the clocks have stopped, but the world is still turning.

We will shine brighter with every lesson we learn during these times. One day the rain clouds will pass and the sun will truly shine. Every storm eventually comes to an end and so will this storm. At the end of the rainbow we can be with our families and friends. We are all in it together.

At the start of 2020 N1 and I were busy preparing poems for a year of brilliant concerts when COVID-19 hit. It seemed the entire world had changed overnight. Fear filled the hearts of billions, a fear driven by the uncertainty of the first global pandemic of our lives.

Before we knew it a whole new language appeared – 'social distancing' and 'self-isolation' – and some of our old language was overused, such as 'unprecedented'. We all had to adjust to a new way of living, and old habits and routines abruptly stopped. We faced the closure of things we enjoy like beaches and cinemas, and even just a cheeky coffee with a friend.

None of this was for nothing. Lives changed, but far worse was the vast loss of life. These tragedies will stay with us forever. The losses have touched us all personally, and it is because of this that we recognise the worth in what we have lost along the way to prevent even more lives being squandered to this pandemic.

Our combined sacrifices are a small part of this. These changes are but a tiny cog in a machine that needed professionals at the frontline to work. Without the NHS, carers, shop workers and many more, our actions would only provide a limited amount of help.

The commute became very different when the pandemic hit London. People were forced, by an invisible danger, to slow down and change the way they use a system that is the core of fast-moving London life. The demand for change was instant and along with national guidance there was an overload of important rules. We knew the mental strain this would have and it was important to recognise and accept that for many this was going to prove very challenging and even become a tipping point for those who were already struggling. It's times like these that togetherness and unity are so important. We felt we could remind many people of that with our boards in the hope of lightening the load and helping to banish isolation from a time that was forcing distance between us all.

Both N1 and I had to work throughout the pandemic. N1 self-isolated for a few weeks with symptoms, but I was fortunate not to have to. Being limited in how we could help in stations was frustrating, and we decided it was important to write messages for the keyworkers to help raise their spirits as well as the nation as a whole at a time when anxiety and mental health problems were rife. We wrote daily boards, even celebrating every birthday, for two months for those who were locked in.

We hope this chapter is a reminder of this period, when words of hope and heroes emerged to keep us all going during one of our darkest periods in recent history.

Service information

THIS IS A WARNING
TO ALL OF OUR FAMILIES
AND FRIENDS IN THE
WORLD,
IT'S SOME IMPORTANT
INFORMATION THAT
YOU NEED TO KNOW;
WHEN THIS IS ALL OVER
YOU'RE GETTING THE
BIGGEST HUGS EVER
AND WE ARE NEVER
GOING TO LET GO.

@allontheboard

Service information

Date **MISSING TOUCH**

Time A POEM INSPIRED BY THE WORDS
OF A 7 YEAR OLD CHILD IN LOCKDOWN

I FEEL SCARED AND WORRIED BECAUSE I MISS MY FRIENDS
AND I DON'T THINK I WILL BE AS HAPPY AS I WAS BEFORE THE VIRUS,
I CAN'T PLAY TAG OR ANY OF THE OLD GAMES WE USED TO PLAY;
I CAN'T GIVE HIGH FIVES, SHAKE HANDS OR HUG MY FAMILY
AND FRIENDS,
I FEEL LIKE I'M TRAPPED IN A BIG CAGE AND I WANT TO FLY AWAY.

I MISS HAVING ADVENTURES INTO THE UNKNOWN
AND PLACES I'VE NEVER BEEN,
I MISS HAVING PLAY DATES WITH MY MATES AND SLEEPOVERS TOO;
I FEEL ANXIOUS AND SAD AT THE SAME TIME
AND I'M MISSING TOUCH SO MUCH,
I HOPE THE VIRUS STOPS SO I CAN GET BACK TO DOING
WHAT I USED TO DO.

@allontheboard

Service information

Date **CAPTAIN**

Time **TOM MOORE**

by @allontheboard

TRUE HEROES EMERGE AS WE TRY TO FLATTEN THE CURVE,

WE SHOULD ALL TRY TO BE MORE LIKE CAPTAIN TOM MOORE;

HE HAS RAISED MILLIONS OF POUNDS FOR NHS HEROES SO FAR,

HE'S A NINETY NINE YEAR OLD SOON TO BE

A ONE HUNDRED YEAR OLD SUPERSTAR,

A NATIONAL TREASURE, A LEGEND AND A VETERAN OF

THE SECOND WORLD WAR.

ACHIEVING WELL DESERVED ACCOLADES AND FAME,

SURELY A KNIGHTHOOD AWAITS,

FOR EACH LAP THE CAPTAIN WALKS

MAY HE FEEL OUR SUPPORT

WITH EVERY LENGTH;

INSPIRING A NATION TO MAKE GENEROUS DONATIONS

WITH HIS POSITIVITY AND SHEER DETERMINATION,

WE SALUTE YOU CAPTAIN TOM MOORE,

THANK YOU FOR YOUR SPIRIT AND STRENGTH.

@allontheboard

Service information

Date

Time

CLAP FOR THE NHS, THE SHOPWORKERS, THE TRANSPORT STAFF,
CLAP FOR THE HEALTH CARERS TOO;
CLAP FOR THE FRONTLINE STAFF, THE SCIENTISTS,
    THE PHARMACIES AND ALL THE KEY WORKERS,
CLAP FOR EVERYTHING THEY CONTINUE TO DO.
CLAP FOR THE VOLUNTEERS AND EVERYONE IN ISOLATION,
CLAP FOR HUMANITY AND THOSE WE HOLD DEAR;
CLAP FOR OURSELVES, ONE ANOTHER AND OUR NEIGHBOURS,
CLAP FOR THE NATION AND THE WORLD TO HEAR.

LOVE @allontheboard

Service information

Date

Time

At this moment in time there are superheroes
                    without capes amongst us;
From working in hospitals and care homes
              to driving an ambulance, a train
                              or a bus.
On train and Tube stations and in shops selling food
                          and stacking shelves;
In GP and dentist surgeries and pharmacies
    looking after us and helping us to take care of ourselves.

The post office workers and delivery drivers,
        the engineers fixing each emergency repair;
Teachers educating key workers children and
                social care workers giving care.
The cleaners who keep cleaning and
        the emergency services and the military
                    responding to every call;
From the farmers to Captain Tom Moore and
    the researchers and scientists trying to find a cure
As we fight an invisible enemy in this war,
        <u>YOU</u> are heroes, one and all.

@allontheboard

Service information

WE CAN'T CONTROL WHAT'S
HAPPENING IN THE WORLD
AT THE MOMENT,
WE CAN'T CONTROL THE LIES
AND THE TRUTH;
BUT, WE CAN CONTROL WHAT
WE DECIDE TO DO WITH
OUR TIME,
BETWEEN OUR OWN FOUR WALLS
AND THE ROOF.
WE CAN'T CONTROL PEOPLE'S
BEHAVIOUR,
WE CAN'T CONTROL WHAT
OTHERS DO AND HOW THEY LIVE;
BUT, WE CAN CONTROL HOW
MUCH NEWS WE WATCH AND
LISTEN TO,
BY DOING THINGS WE ENJOY
INDOORS AND NOT FOCUSING
ON THE NEGATIVE. *@allontheboard*

Service information

Sometimes we need to
take moments to chill,
When we are struggling and
we temporarily lose the tools
that help us to heal.
It seems like the clocks
have stopped and yet
the world will still turn,
We will come back stronger
and shine brighter
with every lesson we learn.
It's perfectly normal to feel
sad and to have a bad day,
But, this won't last forever.
It won't always be this way.

@allontheboard

Service information

During these times
it will be an
impossible task,
for someone who
reads lips to read lips
if we are socially
distancing and wearing
a mask;
We are all in this
together so learning
some sign language or
a new way to communicate
isn't too much to ask.

@allontheboard

Service information

At the moment we may be
limited in what we can do.
But, there is nothing limited
about me and you.
If you're not feeling groovy,
play games, watch TV or
                    a movie
and use the time for creativity.
Write stories or a diary,
learn new skills and exercise,
you're not alone in
                    feeling anxiety.
Use social media as a way
to communicate with others.
In the future there will be
time to enjoy the lovely weather.
it's okay to not be okay,
but, at the end of the day,
It's for the best and
We shall get through this together.

@allontheboard

UNDERGROUND **Service information**

Date **NHS**

Time

By @allontheboard

WE ARE SO GRATEFUL AND TRULY APPRECIATE EVERYTHING YOU DO;
YOU ARE ALL SELFLESS, HARD WORKING SUPERHEROES WITHOUT CAPES,
WHERE WOULD WE BE WITHOUT YOU?

YOU ARE THE HEARTBEAT AND THE BLOOD OF THIS NATION,
YOU LOOK AFTER US AND DO YOUR BEST TO KEEP US ALIVE;
THROUGH ANY DIFFICULT SITUATION YOU SHOW NO DISCRIMINATION,
GIVING EVERYTHING YOU'VE GOT TO HELP SOMEONE SURVIVE.

WE NEED TO PROTECT YOU AND SUPPORT YOU BY STAYING AT HOME,
EVERY SINGLE SACRIFICE YOU ARE ALL MAKING WE WILL
                                    NEVER FORGET;
WE ARE SO LUCKY TO HAVE YOU, YOU DESERVE THE WORLD
                                    AND EVEN MORE,
WE WILL ALWAYS BE FOREVER IN YOUR DEBT.

Love @allontheboard

Service information

The day of your dreams may
          have been cancelled
And this pandemic has ruined
          the wedding you had planned;
For better or worse you may
          be feeling cursed,
If you're feeling upset and frustrated
          everyone can understand.
At the moment you may not know
          when your big day is happening,
Everything you worked so hard for
          has been left in the lurch.
From the food to the guests,
  the reception and the honeymoon,
The venues be it a place that you love,
          a registry office or a church.
Money may have been lost,
          but, true love has no cost,
This won't last forever and there
          will be a light after this gloom.
Someday this situation will end and
  you can get married in front of
                    family and friends,
It will be an even more special day
when the flowers truly bloom.

UNDERGROUND

Service information

Date
Time

VE DAY 75

Many of us today would not
be free or be alive,
Without their sacrifice and
the loss of so many lives
Between 1939 and 1945;
We recognise the bravery of
the greatest generation
of Britons who ever lived and
the debt we owe.
Even though we can not rejoice
In the streets with jubilation
During this coronavirus situation,
United as a nation we
Come together from our homes
To pay respect with gratitude
and celebration;
A Victory over tyranny and the day the guns fell silent
across Europe 75 years ago.

@allontheboard

Service information

Date

Time

IT'S HEARTBREAKING
LOOKING AT THE STATISTICS
FROM ALL OVER THE WORLD
KNOWING THEY ARE
NOT JUST CHARTS OR
NUMBERS ON A LIST;
EACH ONE IS A PERSON
WITH A NAME WHO HAS
LOST THEIR LIFE DURING
THESE TIMES, LEAVING THEIR
GRIEVING LOVED ONES BEHIND,
THEY WILL BE FOREVER LOVED
AND ALWAYS MISSED.

@allontheboard

Service information

I miss the friday feeling,
I even miss the
      monday morning blues;
I miss the escapism of
cinema, sports and travelling
I miss not feeling anxious
while obsessively
      checking the news.
I miss hugging, high fives
      and shaking hands,
I miss being with my
      family and friends;
Never again will I take
anyone or anything for granted,
I will embrace the human race
when this ends. @allontheboard

N I - A THANK YOU

This is our first book so I would like to take the opportunity to thank all of these marvellous people.

Salene, thanks for being my everything, giving me everything and always being there for me. I was born to love you and you have mesmerised me since the first time I saw you. You continue to inspire me everyday. I could write a billion poems for you and I still wouldn't run out of things to say about how wonderful you are and how much you mean to me. I love you. Mum and Dad, thanks for being absolutely amazing since the day I was born. You put a roof over my head when I was growing up and you continue to protect me with your love. I know I will always have a home in your hearts. You made my childhood magic, you have filled my brain with so many wonderful memories and have allowed me to be a dreamer. Thanks for being so easy to love and for loving me (even when I've been a pain in the neck).

Thank you to Nicola, Ben, Ellie (I told you I would mention you in the book. You owe me chocolate), Reiss, Susie, Kason and to all my beautiful family and friends. Thanks for being you and putting up with me. Also sending love to my loved ones and pets in Heaven. I will never forget you and will see you up there one day.

A special thanks to everyone who has followed us since 2017. You truly mean the world to us and this would not have happened without you. You have literally made our dreams come true.

And last, but certainly not least, we would both like to say thank you to YOU. Yes we mean YOU. Thank you so much for buying our book and we hope you find it as wonderful as we find you. Thank you also to Maria King, E.L. James, Millie Hoskins, all the wonderful people at Yellow Kite Books, TfL and everyone who has for helped All On The Board on our journey.

EI - A THANK YOU

To Kasia, Luna and Liam, thank you for your love, support, strength and patience. You have given me love I never thought I would be so lucky to receive. You are the opera in me, the unbreakable strength in my heart. You are my everything. I love you all.

To Mum and Dad, thank you for bringing me into the world, protecting me, teaching me to be kind and to fight for those who are less fortunate than me. Thank you for providing for me and showing me what's right and wrong. I love you both.

To my fabulous friends Carrie, Warren, Fabian and Kevin, who have been part of my creative growth for many years, thank you. To my family and friends in Heaven. I miss you all every day. To my Uncle Dilbagh, I know you would have found all of this quite something so I look forward to sharing it with you one day. To Maria King, our wonderful manager at work when we started this whole thing. You pointed us towards each other and your support will never be forgotten. To E.L. James. Thank you for your advice and your support at a point where we were walking blind. You didn't have to help two strangers but you chose to and that truly spoke volumes.

To everyone at Yellow Kite; Lauren, Jenny, Caitriona, Holly, Abi, thank you all for believing in us, working with us and not giving up when you could have. You are all simply wonderful. Thank you also to everyone at TSBA who worked their magic to keep this project alive and of course to TfL and all those who have supported our work. To Ann Gavaghan, thank you for being there whenever we needed you, you have been a saviour and are a fabulous person through and through. To our agent Millie Hoskins, thank you for joining this adventure with us and working tirelessly to keep our path clear and fair. I look forward to the future with you.

To our followers, we cannot thank you enough for the time you give us. We are humbled by your continued presence and wonderful words of love for what we do. We hope this book is as beautiful as all of you. And to the person reading this right now. I hope this book inspires you to make your own dreams come true. No matter what obstacles you may face, never give up on your dreams, you are worthy of them. Thank you for being a part of ours.

First published in Great Britain in 2020 by Yellow Kite
An imprint of Hodder & Stoughton
An Hachette UK company

9

Copyright © 2020 Ian Redpath and Jeremy Chopra trading as All On The Board

Design by Hart Studio

Cover illustration by Jordan Andrew Carter

Author photo p. 11 by Max Rose-Fyne

Illustration based on photograph of Patrick Hutchinson carrying an injured
counter-protester to safety, near the Waterloo station during a Black Lives
Matter protest © REUTERS/Dylan Martinez

A CIP catalogue record for this title is available from the British Library.

Hardback ISBN 978 1 473 69124 7
eBook ISBN 978 1 473 69125 4

Colour origination by Altaimage London
Printed and bound in Italy by Graphicom Srl

Hodder & Stoughton policy is to use papers that are natural, renewable
and recyclable products and made from wood grown in sustainable forests.
The logging and manufacturing processes are expected to conform to the
environmental regulations of the country of origin.

Yellow Kite
Hodder & Stoughton Ltd
Carmelite House
50 Victoria Embankment
London EC4Y 0DZ

www.yellowkitebooks.co.uk